Fly-Fisher

by the same author

WHALE
THE LONGEST FLIGHT
FUR

Fly-Fisher

JEREMY LUCAS

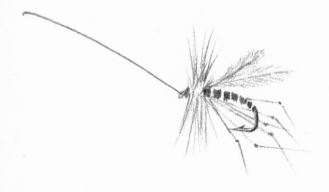

JONATHAN CAPE
THIRTY-TWO BEDFORD SQUARE
LONDON

First published 1986
Copyright © 1986 by Jeremy Lucas

Jonathan Cape Ltd, 32 Bedford Square, London WC1B 3EL

British Library Cataloguing in Publication Data
Lucas, Jeremy
Fly-fisher
1. Trout fishing   2. Fly fishing
799.1'755   SH687
ISBN 0–224–02402–7

Phototypeset by Falcon Graphic Art Ltd
Wallington, Surrey
Printed in Great Britain by
Thomson Litho Ltd, East Kilbride

To my daughters, Hannah and Eleanor,
that when they are adult
the fly-fisher's tale will still be
worth the telling

Contents

Introduction   ix

Part One   Masters of the Nymph   I

1 Man and Method   3

2 A Change of Direction   12

3 Into the Cold   21

4 Long Days, Fair Winds   40

5 Cool Mists and Quick Storms   56

Part Two   Wild Waters   63

6 Into the Hills   65

7 Valley Lochs and the Classic Style   87

8 The Sea-Trout Lochs   108

9 The Way Ahead   132

Appendix   138

Bibliography   145

Illustrations

between pp 38 and 39

1   Sunset at Grafham
2   Stuart Broadhurst at Bewl Water
3   Brown trout ready for the net
4-5 Brown trout, Bewl Water
6   Rainbow trout, Bewl Water
7   Winter on Bewl Water, 1985-6
8   Loch Maree, *c.* 1930
9   Loch Maree from 1,200 feet, 1980

between pp 102 and 103

10   *Salar*, Boat Bay, Loch Maree
11   Cock sea-trout, Loch Maree
12   Loch Hope and Ben Hope from the north
13   Herbert Macdonald, Loch Hope
14   Salmon and sea-trout, Loch Hope
15   Salmon on the dap, Loch Hope
16   Graeme Longmuir and ghillie, Loch Horisary
17   Salmon at the Borgie Falls
18   Sea-trout about to be returned

Introduction

THE OLD COLONEL sat back in his chair and beamed at me.

'Hm,' he uttered, nodding his head, 'that *was* a fine day. You're useful with the oars: good drifting.' He eased his weary bones into the leather upholstery and lit his pipe. 'Could have done with you, forty years ago, at – '

'No, Colonel, I would have been scared out of my wits. Besides,' I hurriedly reminded him, 'I wasn't even alive then.'

'Hm.' He had been at the malt since dinner time. I was sure he was going to tell me another war story.

'Do you know, I haven't felt so *alive* since the Bridge.' His eyes glazed and I thought he had slipped back through the years to relive the time when he and a brave few had taken on the German tanks. 'That fish', he continued, 'was astonishing. It just came out of nowhere and hit that fly like . . . ' He struggled for an appropriate simile.

'Like a Panzer division?' I suggested.

'More like the whole bloody Third Reich!'

Thus a single 6-lb sea-trout had fired the old campaigner's imagination more than anything else in forty full years. He would take with him the memory of the Bridge and the big fish to the grave. I understood that; the heroics of the one and the thrill of both.

I might have been too young for the tanks, but for twenty years trout have certainly filled much of my time.

INTRODUCTION

Fly-fishing is an intensely personal sport and each of us seeks from it different pleasures and goals. One comes to realise that the doctrines of self-appointed experts are often inconsistent with one's own humble philosophy, and that they are, finally, inconsequential.

If we scan fly-fishing literature over the last decade, we see that the craft has evolved considerably in that time. It might be said that we are in the midst of a renaissance. With the sheer area of widely available water in the British Isles, an increasing number of fly-fishers are seeking values previously upheld only to a small extent. The search ends with the individual and, more frequently now on our stillwaters, we find fishers who have come to accept that catching trout is not difficult; the trick is to take on the challenge through self-imposed limitations. This book is about my own experiences within such a framework; the men who have helped me develop it, the environments in which it is practised and the trout towards which it is targeted. I thought it was a fine thing to write about.

Part One

Masters of the Nymph

I

Man and Method

ON THE SURFACE he came at the fly. There was no mad
rush, no massive expenditure of energy; just a peaceful
sweep of his great tail. In the early dusk off Grudie Point,
Loch Maree, the huge trout wallowed, like a U-boat in the
swell. I had already had a five-pounder earlier in the week;
but this fish was more than twice that weight, probably
around 12 lbs. He was a sea-trout, his thick, silver flesh
strewn with big black dots. The kype on his lower jaw
was as big as a man's thumb. He was an almost impossible
prize and he had nearly reached the fly, a Claret Pennell on
the top dropper, dibbling across the waves. My mind's
camera was on power-drive, click, click, click, and I can
see the frames now; the immense flashing shape bearing
down on my fly, and the setting sun and the golden waves
reflecting the faces of reddened mountains. Then, a second
before that cavernous mouth would have engulfed my
offering, a sea-trout of 1½ lbs whirled out of the deep,

snatched the fly and leapt off across the loch. I clearly recall the big trout, his target suddenly stolen by the young fish, turning down lethargically towards his resting place off the Point, the wide shovel of his tail sliding above the surface as if to say goodbye. I remember the agony and the thrill. It is for moments such as this that a fly-fisher lives.

Pursuing trout with a fly is a way of life. There are those, I suppose, who only occasionally pull out an old fly rod from the spare room, place it carelessly with a leaky pair of waders in the boot of the car and merely toy with the idea of using it on a forthcoming holiday; but among the growing numbers of those who call themselves fly-fishers I have rarely met the man or woman of casual approach. No, the hunt for trout is a force which pulses in the blood, fills the mind with nostalgic recollection and new hopes. It drives one to holiday in remote and wild places, even to live there, for a trout fisher yearns to be a part of the environment he loves above all others. An occasional visit is not enough, indeed it is masochistic, for to leave the mountains and the windswept lochs, to turn one's back on a river fining down from spate, strikes a deep pain into the man with a rod. To say goodbye with no certainty of early return is worst of all.

So it is for the many thousands of men like me for whom I write: all those who, long before winter is gone, spend hours at the vice dressing flies. Even before the buds of chestnut and birch have begun to swell, the rods are all cleaned after their last busy season, the lines are treated and lovingly wound on to well-oiled reels. New false leaders are tied on, coats, waders and overtrousers are checked for wear; all is made ready while our quarry feels no change in the cold waters. He has barely moved from the loch's depths since the November breeding run. He waits, and his hunters watch the lengthening dusks, dreaming of winds from the west.

Someone made a very bad mistake when I was young, for I was given a fishing rod. Quite early on I graduated to a fly rod and have never looked back. Yes, it has become a way of life, only hindered by the requirements of a long-suffering family and the need to make a living. But my wife made the biggest mistake of all in marrying a man whose life was to be split between travelling to wild places in the north-west and spending what time was left in the study – for my other love is writing. She tells me, however, that she does not *really* need holidays in sun-soaked regions and she loves the kick of the boat on the storm-tossed waves of Loch Maree, so the family survives. None the less, there are those moments of my guilt when she turns her eyes to heaven and exclaims: 'Oh not again, you've been out every day for the past week!' Sheepishly I back my way to the car, making promises I rarely fulfil.

But when I reach the loch or lake shore the stinging reprimand, 'When are to going to spend some time with us?' and the plaintive, 'How will we ever earn any money?' have become whispers. The wind builds and waves chatter against the boat's hull. I hear only these sounds and see only sea-trout flipping up out of the water against a back-drop of mountains and ancient Scots pine. And I feel nothing more than the intense urge to catch these magnificent fish.

Here I must make a statement of contrition. There is, probably, something fundamentally wrong about killing. At its most base level fly-fishing is a blood sport. What I hope to show is that it stands apart from all others. Within the framework of changing attitudes as regards sport for enjoyment and aesthetic interpretation, a breed of hunter is evolving who cares as much for the fish as for the fishing. Today the man with a fly rod seeks to protect those environments through which he passes. He is a conser-

5

vationist with a rich understanding of water systems, and
he, more often than not, has a hand in directly nurturing
their sensitive ecology. The hazards facing freshwaters are
due to other causes, which I shall show later. It is doubtful
that those of us who wish to see the continuation of
wildernesses can make amends for the havoc wrought by
other human activity.

Trout fishing is a broad term. Fly-fishing is more
definitive and it is entirely within the bounds of catching
trout with an artificial fly that this book is concerned.
Furthermore, I will consider only those sections of the
sport which may be regarded as being truly representative,
for the term 'fly-fishing' has, since the 1960s, become an
umbrella term to include fishing with a lure and even
trolling with lead-cored and high-density lines.

It is sad that fishing the lure has become so popular on
English stillwaters, not only because it takes trout which
would otherwise be caught by more subtle methods, but
also because it robs its users of the real and lasting joys of
true fly-fishing. I know only too well that there are days
when to fish a nymph, dry or traditional wet fly will result
in a catch less heavy than that produced by the lure fishers;
but these days are the exceptions. Over the duration of a
season a lure will take fewer trout than a competent
nymph fisher. I have seen this proved time after time. It
cannot be questioned that the latter will have to apply his
mind more; but this is precisely where the satisfaction lies.
Of course it is easier to fish a lure, once the use of a
powerful rod and shooting head line has been mastered. I
write from unpleasant experience. For a few years at the
end of the 1960s and early 1970s I experimented with the
lure and although I made some huge catches, including
some very large brown and rainbow trout, not a single one
of these has been recorded in the log and I remember very
little about them. Luckily I was rescued by Peter Grundel

6

and Arthur Cove who educated me in the ways of trout with the nymph – and that was the biggest breakthrough in my career on the English fisheries. What all this amounts to is that to me, and any resolute fly-fisher, a thousand trout taken on a lure represent just a thousand dead fish, while the one trout which falls to a nymph or traditional wet fly fished in the proper manner is a very special creature indeed.

Let us not wonder at the numbers that are caught, or even how big they are, rather at *how* they are caught. For thousands of fly-fishers this statement has formed what has become an axiom by which their approach to the sport is governed. There are other fundamental principles, but none so sacrosanct as this.

This book is concerned with the two main species of trout; *salmo trutta* (the brown trout and its migratory cousin the sea-trout) and *salmo gardinari* (the rainbow trout). That *salmo salar*, the Atlantic salmon, also lunges up from the deep from time to time is something for which I make no apology; salmon are often encountered when one is sea-trout or brown trout fishing and they add further excitement to a day on the loch.

Where I like best to hunt for these fish is on stillwaters. In England the larger the lake the better, for the bigger they are the more they resemble the vast Highland lochs which are my first love. So most of my fishing nowadays, when south of the border, is on Bewl Bridge in Kent, Grafham Water in Cambridgeshire (formerly Hunting-donshire) and, increasingly, Rutland Water in Leicester-shire (formerly Rutland). These happen to be three of the finest rainbow trout fisheries in Europe and their brown trout fishing, particularly Grafham's and Rutland's, is also superb. Bewl is the smallest of these at 770 acres, Grafham occupies 1,700 acres, while Rutland covers 3,100 acres – 10 per cent of the old county of Rutland. I have been lucky enough to have fished dozens of other stillwaters in England, large and small, ranging from the lovely lakes of Cornwall – Sibblyback and rugged Crowdy, to Draycote and multi-armed Pitsford in the Midlands, to Ardleigh in Essex which I remember as a fine water for brown trout. (The methods I describe on the three main lakes of my choice have worked equally well on any of those I have visited.) And I shall go on searching for fresh challenges, as long as I am able, but I doubt that I shall ever find anywhere to match Grafham and Rutland – to me the king and queen of English trout fisheries, and Bewl, the beautiful princess.

Years ago I used to do more fishing on rivers, especially in Scotland, Cornwall and then on the chalk in the south-east; but when challenged by lakes like Grafham and more particularly the lochs of Wester Ross and Sutherland, my loyalties were inexorably shifted. One must simply follow one's soul and mine rests by the big waters.

All this leads me to what must be the ultimate in fly-fishing: the large sea-trout lochs and the thousands of lochs that lie scattered over the Hebrides and far north of Scotland. Here is a fly-fisher's paradise and here too occur those thrilling encounters with grilse and salmon. For me the pinnacle must be the treasured drifts of Maree and Hope; and these I shall refer to in detail later.

Now that the arena and the opponent have been outlined, the methods and weapons should be examined. I have long since outgrown the need to encumber myself with bags full of heavy tackle. I have fished a great deal and many years ago found the tools with which I was most comfortable. Of all the rods that I have used, I now restrict myself to only two. One is a custom-built nine-foot carbon fibre Fibatube rated to carry an AFTM #6 line, but on which I use a #5 double taper line; the other is a ten-foot Fibatube in the same material rated at #4/5/6, on which I also load a #5 double taper.

The lines, like the rods, are of paramount importance. For nearly all my fishing I use an Aircel Supreme or a Cortland 444, both floaters and both #5. Until the end of the 1985 season I often preferred a dressed Kingfisher silk line, number 2, which is equivalent to #5, when drifting for sea-trout with the long rod. With their long tapers and fine diameters, and the beautiful translucence of the natural material, I believe these lines were the finest ever made for traditional wet fly fishing. Sadly, Kingfisher no longer exists and the lines are extinct. My last one became too frail and broke on a big Maree sea-trout. But the modern lines are almost as good, despite their opacity and thickness, and we should not mourn the loss of Kingfisher too long. (I am told that a company in the Midlands has begun to produce silk lines, but I have not yet seen one.)

With the use I give it, a line usually lasts only a single season. The Cortland does last a little longer, but the Aircel is slightly better for long-distance casting. With both lines, loaded on the nine-foot rod, casts of thirty yards or more are easily achieved in anything but the most unfavourable winds. As with the rods, I have tried other lines, though I have found none better than these two. Shooting heads and forward taper lines, of course, make it easier to achieve long casts, but they are inferior in presenting and working a nymph, wet or dry fly. Furthermore, I happen to believe that weight-forwards should be limited to inexperienced casters or to extremely inclement conditions. One does not meet many experienced nymph fishers who need such lines to achieve long distances. One soon finds harmony with a double taper.

The reader will have noticed that I frequently refer to floating or 'dry' lines; this is purely a personal thing. Wet or sinking lines tend towards that other pet hate of mine:

the lure. Besides, the floater is the most versatile of lines, as I shall show.

The reels are simple and again I know of none better than the Hardy Marquis with its exposed rim (which should never be touched when a big fish is running – as I learnt to my cost when I tried to slow down the biggest salmon I ever hooked on the River Helmsdale). They are now made with silent checks, which eliminates that sometimes annoying ratchet. I use a #7 which allows plenty of backing behind a #5 line. This really is necessary for salmon, sea-trout and even some of the Grafham fish. As recently as the 1985 season, a rainbow on Grafham's west bank stripped off the fly line and fifty yards of backing on his first rush – and he weighed only 2¼ lbs! On the same day Peter Grundel, my long-standing companion at Grafham, had a similar thing happen to him with a trout of equal size.

Now, enough said about such matters, for every serious fly-fisher is married to his own equipment, and this is how it should be. I have only mentioned mine because it is of such importance to my discussion of the various styles of fly-fishing.

The most versatile method is the traditional wet fly, which is the backbone of the sport in the British Isles. When boat fishing it is the method I use nearly all the time. This ancient approach of our forefathers is related to the other main style which is merely a highly adapted development of the traditional wet. I refer to the nymph. This method is the one I use for certain Scottish lochs where the brown trout seem to take the nymph better than traditional patterns. It is on the big English lakes, however, that this style comes into its own, and it is fished best from the bank, or from a boat which is at anchor – a drifting boat cries out for the traditional wet. Both these approaches to trout I shall detail in their relevant chapters, together with more occasional methods such as dry fly, dapping and various combinations.

Technicalities, however, should not be our concern here, for they are far too over-worked in trout fishing literature. It takes a long time, I know, to learn that fly-fishing is a simple and uncluttered art. If performed well it is always fluent and graceful. It requires much thought and endless practice, but it is nevertheless closer to art than science. It excites the primordial instincts in a man and it is the development of these that determines how successful he is with a fly rod. The brilliant science that has gone into the making of fine, modern tackle helps us to catch trout, but those men, now dead, with their silk lines, horsehair casts and greenheart rods were also successful. The ancient instincts are what matter, and the modern approach to conservation.

In the following pages I have collected together some of the images and memories, as well as details from the log, and set everything down in the hope that it helps a fly-fisher not necessarily to catch more trout, but to understand a little better the styles, the challenges and the trout themselves, and especially the immeasurable value of those beautiful places in the British Isles where trout exist.

2

A Change of Direction

'COME ON THE BANK, where the men fish,' said Arthur Cove to me one day a long time ago. Tentatively, I did as I was told. He was referring to the banks of Grafham Water which was then the mecca of fly-fishing for rainbow trout in Europe and thus was the pride of the Anglian Water Authority in whose area it lies. Grafham is challenged now by one or two other waters, notably Rutland. In those days, however, there were no contenders. The name was on every fly-fisher's lips and they came from all over the British Isles, even Scotland, from France, Germany and Holland, and a few from the United States where the rainbow trout is common; and none went away unimpressed.

Grafham first opened for fly-fishing in the last half of the 1966 season. It has changed considerably in the twenty years since then, but so do all lakes as they evolve. The trees are taller now and soften its once harsher shores. The banks have become undermined by erosion, particularly along the north shore where the south-west winds have driven two decades of waves. The aquatic fly life has altered and with it the character of the trout.

When Grafham reservoir was flooded it drowned 1,700 acres of rich agricultural land. Planktonic life bloomed and insect life was soon established. Evening hatches were astonishing. Adult buzzers, chironomids, hung in clouds like smoke over the bushes. It was as if the trees were on fire. Sedge flies of various species (I particularly remember the silverhorns and longhorns) quickly added themselves to the density of invertebrate life. Nowhere else have I seen hatches like those during Grafham's early years. The trout fed on this plethora of food, and quickly both browns and rainbows became large fish. None of the trout which were put into the reservoir was much heavier than 1 lb in weight. From a stock before the season opened, say in March or April, the fish weighed 2½ lbs by September, some even as much as 3 lbs. Overwintered rainbows were 4 lbs on the opening of the next season and glorious six-pounders before the end. The brown trout did not fare quite so well, for they have slower growth rates. None the less weight gains occurred of a pound or more a year. This rapid growth was a phenomenon and would have been enough on its own to put Grafham on the map.

There was more. The heavy trout were free risers. It must be said that they were usually very easy to bring to the fly in those days, although, once hooked, they showed their worth. Stories came back to the lodge, and then appeared in the angling press, of 3-lb rainbows that stripped off a hundred yards of line in their first furious dashes. 'Smash takes' were heard of when two-pounders hit a fly with such force that 6- or 7-lb breaking strain leaders gave way. Trout were said to jump a dozen times, their glistening bodies writhing, until they shook themselves free of the hooks that held them. And most of the stories were true. Grafham trout were, and often still are, extraordinarily acrobatic. It would not be too much to say that a legend was in the making, at least among men who knew trout.

During these years, before I met the men who were to change my whole approach to fishing in large reservoirs and lakes, I regularly visited Grafham with my brother-in-law, Johnny. We always fished from the boats. How well I remember those mile-long drifts over the clear, wave-torn water. Johnny comes from another land of trout, southern Ireland, and he tackled Grafham as he would his native loughs. We fished with slow, cane rods and teams of traditional wet flies. The twenty intervening years have not dulled my memory of those early days, for they were as good as all but the best seasons in north-western Scotland. Yes, I was new to English lake fishing and so it was a novel experience; but there we were, entwined with angling history.

None of these memories is more vivid than my first trout on our very first visit. A mile across the water from the lodge we drifted into Hill Farm Bay. The sun was shining and a south wind gently blowing. We had not moved a fish after almost three hours of repetitive casting. We had seen a few rainbows leaping from the surface and I remember thinking that they looked more like fresh-run grilse. It was lunch time. Until then we had been working the flies very high in the water in the hope of attracting one of the big cruising fish. As an experiment I cast as long a line as I could and did not retrieve. The flies sank, the line lay in curves ahead of the boat as we drifted. I recall that the tip of the fly line was sinking. I was watching it when, almost in disbelief, I saw it draw steadily away. Obviously, something was pulling. In shock, I lifted the rod high in the air above and behind me and felt a lovely, heavy weight pulsing through the wood. Johnny, as surprised as I, cried, 'You've got one!' Well, I knew that. We were in shallow water by this time and the trout was swimming in wide circles close to the bottom while the rod took on the bow shape loved by all fly-fishers. After five minutes of concentrated nerve-tingling as my whole body shook uncontrollably, I managed to ease him to the net, which enabled Johnny to scoop him out of the water. He was a brown trout weighing 1½ lbs and was the most beautiful creature I had ever seen. I caught him on a Teal and Orange and I thought it was the finest fly ever invented.

My mother still has the photograph of me with that fish. I cringe now when I look at it because of the stupid expression on my face, almost split in two by a huge smile. But then I see the trout and I relive those incredible few minutes on the lake, twenty years ago.

As I have said, it was lunch time, though I was too excited to eat anything. With renewed vigour I cast again and again until the late dusk finally vanquished my efforts. I did not catch another fish, but Johnny had three rainbows, the best weighing 3¾ lbs.

The two greatest fishermen in the world took the boat back to the jetty that evening. I weighed the trout, proudly taking my time at the scales while others waited, probably somewhat amused. I barely noticed that everyone else had done as well as we had, several a good deal better. A kind-hearted elderly fisher came over to me.

'You've had a good day then?'

'Oh, not bad,' I replied, 'not bad.' And that was the biggest understatement that has ever passed my lips.

My next Grafham visit is also worth the telling. Again I caught only the one fish which was also a brown trout. Not 200 yards away from where I had taken that very first trout we were once more drifting in towards the bank on a light southerly. The water was crystal clear and I could see the bottom beneath the boat. There were patches of weed on the yellow bed. As on the first visit I cast as far as I could and allowed the flies to sink. This time, instead of watching the fly line, I looked fixedly at the place where I imagined the flies to be. We were only about thirty yards from the shore. I retrieved the slack line and began to lift the flies. Suddenly, from the deep a trout appeared, swimming slightly to the left of the boat towards the bank and about four feet down. I realised it was following the flies. I lifted the rod higher, instinctively giving my offering some motion in order to induce a response from the trout. I saw its fins spread, and the fish seemed to be dancing towards its target, while time stopped still. I saw a flicker of white that was the trout's mouth opening and closing and I knew a fly had been taken. In that same moment I stroked the rod behind me and I had hooked my second Grafham fish.

Much water has passed beneath the countless boats I have hired since those early days. Now, whenever I drive around the dam wall on the road to the fishing lodge and I see Grafham's expanse opening beyond Gaynes Cove I am always warm with nostalgia and those brown trout still flash before my eyes.

Slowly we learnt, building confidence and understanding, and though we had our blank days there were many more on which by dusk we had a good weight of trout in the creel. Grafham, however, was rapidly evolving, the fishing was becoming more of a challenge and we had to apply our hard-earned knowledge to keep pace with the more elusive shoals of rainbows. Sometimes we had no success until those long evenings when trout began to rise at hatching flies.

Then, quite abruptly, Johnny became heavily immersed in his work as a surgeon. He found less time to visit

Grafham. I remember he took a season ticket at Hanning-field in Essex, its closer proximity to home leading him to believe that he would be able to fish there more often. We fished there only twice in that year. This too was a young lake and the fishing for rainbows was easy. It was incomparable to Grafham and still is.

Johnny and I have not fished together on Grafham since that time. Our last trip was disappointing and we shivered with the cold on a bleak spring day struggling for a few fish apiece. Packing up early on that grey afternoon, we drove off with sinking hearts. I looked back over the wind-torn lake, the black scud marks racing towards the far shore. All of its square miles were deserted; and I loved it still. I will be back, I secretly said to Grafham, when I have learnt a bit more.

These were the darkest days of my fishing life, brightened only by a few visits to Scotland with traditional wet fly. For then I was passing through a phase of fishing the lure on English waters which, in the end, was just so much time in the dustbin. There were lessons learnt, I suppose; the effect of a constant retrieve, a trout's trigger response, the essential need to find the right depth, though all these things one learns with a fly. Dark days, when my interest began to wane and I barely appreciated the strange light one sees over a big water in the early morning or late evening, and all that mattered was a heavy bag of fish.

It did not last long, for rescue was close at hand. During these years I used my holidays from school and then university to work in the fishing business. I was a ghillie in Scotland, I dressed salmon and trout flies for sale and I worked for Don's of Edmonton, the largest tackle shop in north London. This was a tremendous step along the road of fly-fishing, for at Don's I was working with true experts in the field, and really, there are very few of those.

17

Don Neish, the proprietor, is one of the most innovative men I have ever known. He had trained as an engineer before moving into the tackle trade. With his inventive mind and skilful hands he has designed several pieces of equipment that have aided fishers around the world. He was a former international tournament caster and when I worked for him he still held two British records.

So my interest was renewed under Don's careful tuition. Abandoning the heavy lines and poker-like rods that had, for a year or two, enabled me to cast reasonable distances, I returned to proper fly tackle. Don had designed a glass-fibre rod called the 'Grafham Ghost'. This tool was a beautiful compromise between power and comfort in use. Though outdated now by the innovation of carbon fibre, the Ghost was in its time one of the finest all-round rods designed for lake trout fishing.

I remember watching Don in admiration as he flexed the Ghost and sent a #6 line snaking off into the far distance, apparently using very little effort. Now here was something I very much wanted to do. He taught me the finer points about the 'double haul' technique for accelerating a line, the narrow loop and Charles Ritz's motto: 'High speed, high line.'

One discovers that the secret lies in the timing. Motion is the key; the line, rod and arm are in perfect harmony and always in motion as energy is transferred from one point to the next.

It is a wonderful experience to break the 'thirty-yard barrier' with a #6 double taper line. Then to be able to do it not one cast in three, or one in two, but every cast, at whim. And finally to do it with an artist's line, a double taper floater no heavier than a #5. Nothing adds more to one's confidence in fly-fishing than being able to extract the very best from light tackle, to lift the line and shoot it out thirty yards, landing a nymph as though it were feather-down in the midst of feeding trout. It is all part of the mystical maze through which trout men must find their way in the hunt for an understanding of rod and line, fish and loch. Trout, being what they are, ensure that we never quite escape the maze's last corridors. The fun would be over were we to do so.

Then, of course, there was Arthur Cove, who is acknowledged as being the finest exponent of the nymph method in this country. After Don's help with the fly rod and line came Arthur's instruction on nymph and trout. 'Come on the bank,' he had said and thus opened for me a whole new arena of fly-fishing.

In the years during which Arthur Cove fished Grafham four or five times a week, Peter Grundel and I often accompanied him. To watch either of these two men was to soak up their watercraft. But among my many faults is my impatience. I could never watch for long. The trout were out there and I had to be among them. While Arthur was, and is, quite obviously a master of the nymph I had at least to try to emulate him.

It can be daunting when faced with a water the size of Grafham to attempt to fish it from the bank. A boat gives mobility and rapid access to any part of the lake, while a bank fisher is comparatively restricted. Therein begins the challenge. Different skills are called for from a boat; but often it is easier to find the fish while afloat and therefore to catch them. Also, it is rarely essential to throw a long line, while from the shore it nearly always is. When presented with the vast area of bank available at any of our large stillwaters (Grafham is ten miles in perimeter, Bewl, owing to its more winding shape, fifteen and Rutland twenty), a fisher must call on all his watercraft and local knowledge in order to assess where the trout will be. This can change from day to day according to the conditions (though in settled weather the shoals of rainbows tend to congregate in certain areas for weeks at a time). Even when a fly-fisher has found his trout, he may yet be using the wrong fly or presenting it at the incorrect depth or speed. These variables, however, apply equally to boat fishing.

It is fortunate for the bank fisher that trout do tend, most of the time, to collect near the shoreline; in shallow water where nymphs and crustacea abound. Given that certainty we can bolster our confidence and begin to read the variable conditions, such as the weather and wind direction, signs of insect or fish activity.

The best way of passing on some of the lessons learnt over years of fishing the nymph is to consider a season in sequence, from cold spring through to the mellow, shortening days of autumn. The following chapters deal with the three phases of a bank fisher's year.

3

Into the Cold

We are at our keenest before the last frosts have left the land. Most stillwaters open for trout fishing in early April, some even at the end of March. In England this is the time of year I like best, and I am always anxious to be at the lakeside again after so long an absence. The anticipation of the first trout of a new season can lead to sleepless nights as the day draws near. What makes matters worse is that I usually miss out the first few days of the season because this is when one finds the only crowds of the year by the southern lakes. Everyone, I suppose, is itching for trout and to drive away winter's cobwebs.

Even in these early days, however, if one is prepared to travel light and walk a long way, a remote bank can be reached where few have trodden since the season before. For the nymph fisher such a place is ideal and it is towards this that he should head. The sun is slow to warm the air in these young spring days; a good walk helps the circulation and puts one in the right frame of mind. Strolling along the shore, gathering information on the way, one is already remembering how deep it is off a particular bank, and where the trout usually lie. Even if the water is unfamiliar, some points and bays look more attractive than others as trout holding areas.

My first trip to Bewl Bridge was on one such raw spring day when a grey sky merged with dark water and the air was cold. Few buds had burst on the trees and everything looked scrubbed clean and barren. I am always comparing one water with another and having had, the previous season, a wonderful time on Grafham and Loch Maree, Bewl looked a poor prospect for happy days ahead. I was alone on a new fishery and as all exploratory trout men know, this can be a humbling experience. Peter had fished there before and he had suggested a few places to try. I took his advice and headed off in the direction of Bramble Point, only half a mile west of the fishing lodge. The walk through that ancient woodland, which extends unbroken for miles around parts of Bewl's shoreline, considerably warmed my spirits.

On reaching Bramble Bay I found half a dozen lure fishers toiling away between the corner of the bay and its mouth, but there was plenty of room and I found a spot at the head of the Point. A gentle breeze was blowing from the north-east. It was half past five in the afternoon. No trout were showing and there was no sign of a buzzer hatch. The fish would be deep; I was going to have to work at it. I tied on a size 8 Pheasant Tail on the point (the largest hook size I ever use) which would sink quickly and a size 10 in the same pattern on a single dropper five feet above the point fly. I had a few tentative casts close in to the bank, but they were brief. It is rarely worth pausing too long in the shallows when the weather is bitterly cold and other fishermen are in the water close by. I waded in, working the line, and was soon fishing a good thirty yards out.

During the first hour I had neither seen a trout on the surface nor had any response to the fly. I had allowed the leader to sink until the heavier Pheasant Tail must have been close to the bottom, and had inched them slowly back. I had tried some fast retrieves in the hope of surprising a cruising fish. At about half past six, as the wind began to drop, I had my first take and missed it. Shortly afterwards I saw one or two rises on the surface. Small black buzzers began to hatch off. I did not change flies because Pheasant Tails are deadly during a rise to buzzers. I had another take and missed that too; but then the first fish took proper hold and I beached it, a 1-lb rainbow, clean and bright. Soon another followed to make the brace. Both fish had taken the larger point nymph.

Well, I had taken my first Bewl Bridge trout, but it had done little more than warm my enthusiasm. I persisted, however, and, as so often happens in the spring, the days improved as I explored that pretty lake's shores. The next trip brought three, including a brown trout of 1½ lbs, and the following visit gave me a 3-lb rainbow as the last fish of a catch of four. I had just beached a smaller trout and the dusk was falling. There were a few rises about twenty yards out. I began to wade in, working out line as I went, intending to make a 'proper' cast in due course. The big fish must have been no more than seven or eight yards from the bank. As I tightened to lift off I hooked him. He had taken the nymph 'on the drop', a frequent, though often unobserved, phenomenon. He was a demon of a trout, and rushed around for ten minutes in the calm water. It was almost dark as I drew him over the rim of the net.

In April, more than in any other month except the dour days of August, one has to take one's chances when they occur. Sometimes the trout begin to feed in earnest on a brief hatch of buzzers and will take an imitation during this period. It may all be over, however, in half an hour. Unless one's fly is in the right place during that brief activity, the best chance of the day will have been missed. There might be another hatch later, often there will not. In cold weather one cannot rely on there being an evening rise. Even when trout are not showing on the surface they may be feeding down below, hidden, wolfing down buzzer pupae rising from the lake bed. The fish may not come within six feet of the surface. They may even remain within inches of the bottom as they feed on buzzer larvae or caddis. On days of very low temperatures or squally conditions when the barometer is low, this is common. Then you will have to fish the size 8 nymph with as heavy a dressing as your principles allow. I never use lead, finding that extra turns of copper wire under the nymph's thorax is quite adequate for fishing the fly close to the bottom in up to fourteen or fifteen feet of water, provided the wind is no stronger than a force 4, or, if from behind, a force 5.

If the nymph's dressing is sparse (which it should be anyway for attracting the trout – many fishers use flies that are far too bulky in the misguided belief that a large mouthful will be more attractive), it will cut through the surface film and sink rapidly. A heavy dropper fly will help in this process. Leader length is of vital importance here. Except when dry fly-fishing or when casting directly into a strong wind, I never use a leader less than fifteen feet long. My standard length is eighteen feet, while in certain conditions it might be as long as twenty-seven. There are several reasons for this. Firstly, I like to fish two or three flies with the droppers placed a good distance apart in order to have them fishing at different depths. Secondly, the fly line can scare established trout, especially the white lines so favoured by nymph men. It is best, therefore, to have the flies as far away from the line tip as is reasonably possible. Lastly, with a short leader on a floating line, it is impossible to achieve sufficient depth; with a long leader the point fly, at least, can usually be presented on the bottom if this proves necessary.

Another factor in our pursuit of depth is the leader material. Nylon monofilament is naturally rather buoyant. Some makes are worse than others. The best I have used is manufactured by the German company Bayer. It is available wound on either a red or blue spool. The blue is shiny and flashes in the sunlight and I would not dare put it near a wild trout. The material on the red spool, however, is dull, can be made to sink very easily and is utterly reliable. Platil, another German company, also produce an excellent nylon, and Sylcast is a good third choice. Only if I could not find any of these three would I fish with anything else.

The breaking strain of the leader is the last important factor in consideration of this point and here we are always compromising. The thinner the nylon, the faster it can be made to sink; but to set a size 8 hook in a trout's bony mouth with anything less than a 5-lb breaking strain line is risky. Added to this is the fact that we often have twenty to thirty-five yards of fly line on the water. The combined thrust of a quickly moving fish, the weight of fly line and the force of any strike is inviting a break. And that is a great sin in trout fishing. A fish with a hook in certain parts of its mouth will probably die and the end will not come quickly. That trout may struggle for days to rid itself of the hook. Finally beaten by pain, exhaustion, loss of blood or infection, it succumbs. Images such as this are the darkest side of fly-fishing. It is my firm belief that the killing is not nearly as bad as the suffering; but the kill must be quick and clean.

For this style of fishing with the deep nymph, therefore, 5 lbs breaking strain must be the minimum or 4 lbs if a braided leader or shock absorber is used in the butt. On a stormy day 6 lbs is better. Leader material is important in another sense, in that the heavier the strain, the thicker it is. If the line is too thick it is highly visible and I am convinced that this can frighten a trout. I remember a day at Bewl which strengthened my view on this matter. Stuart Broadhurst, another of my regular companions, and I were fishing side by side, both presenting the same nymphs to a dense shoal of rainbow trout. Within an hour I had caught six trout and had numerous takes. Stuart, meanwhile, had not had a single offer. We examined his tackle and all looked well until we noticed that his leader stood out like rope in the water. It was the same 5 lbs breaking strain as my own, but a different make. He changed to the same material that I had been using and immediately began to catch trout. Arthur Cove holds the opposite view. He believes that fish see the leader but do not associate it with danger. I accept the possibility but both of us have had experiences which support our own arguments.

All this talk about depth might lead one to suppose that April necessitates a nymph close to the lake bed. Trout are opportunistic feeders. If there is any insect or plankton activity close to the surface trout will usually be there to harvest it. When no sign of fish is observed it is all too easy to assume that they are deep. But trout are creatures of the light and only the largest of their kind skulk for any length of time in deep, dark water. Even on the coldest, wildest days there are usually some trout braving the surface layers. Rainbow trout in particular are avaricious hunters. Their shoals patrol wide areas of the lake in a search for food between the surface and the bottom, *usually* at depths of no more than twelve or fourteen feet.

If one sees no activity at all, it is probably best to fish the deep nymph, on the long leader, retrieving slowly, often simply allowing a side-wind to impart any necessary motion to the flies. But then nothing might happen for some time or a fish might be caught on one of the droppers which indicates activity in the mid-depths.

There are two approaches to properly presenting a fly between the surface and a depth of, say, six feet. One is to continue using heavier nymphs and retrieving them quickly in order to keep them higher in the water. The other is to change down to size 12s, 14s and 16s which will not sink so rapidly and may be retrieved more slowly. The choice of method depends on the trout and the nature of the food forms causing the activity. Sometimes both methods will work, often only one or the other.

An experience I had at Grafham about six years ago comes immediately to mind. Peter Grundel and I were fishing in one of the bays along the north bank two weeks after the season had opened. We had been there for an hour or two when an enormous shoal of rainbows began to move in the heavy swell. They were rising with that characteristic unhurried, porpoise-like roll as they took black buzzer nymphs from the top few inches of water. Logically, I thought, I tied a size 12 Pheasant Tail on the point and two size 12 Black Buzzers on droppers. I cast among the trout and retrieved slowly. Peter, close by, had continued with larger nymphs. He retrieved more quickly and had caught seven trout before I had had a take! At last I managed to land one of my buzzers on a fish's nose and I had him. Peter, meanwhile, was battling with his eighth catch. I changed to a larger nymph on the point and a fast retrieve and, the very next cast, was into my second.

To consolidate this experience was another which occurred at Bewl Bridge when Stuart and I were enjoying our first visit of the 1985 season. Occasional trout were moving in the waves and I was drifting small nymphs in a fairly strong left to right wind. Stuart was using a large nymph and drawing it in quickly, much too quickly.

'Damn,' I heard him mutter, 'missed it!' He's imagining things I thought. Then, a few casts later, he claimed to have missed another.

'Nonsense,' I replied, 'you're retrieving too fast.'

He fumed behind the smoke from his pipe. 'I know it looks like that, but it's how they want it.'

On the very next cast he proved his point and took our first trout of the season, a lovely, silver rainbow. 'Why don't you try pulling the flies in instead of all that bloody stupid pretty stuff on the drift?' he announced cruelly. I did as he so rudely suggested, caught a trout and we both laughed.

As often as not, however, trout will give no response to a quickly moving nymph and will take one that is barely drifting where the wind carries it. One has to experiment to find the mood of the moment. The fly-fisher's mind is never inactive.

The choice of nymphs, the delicate contact between trout and man, is as important in the spring as at any time of year. The selection, however, is simpler now than it becomes from early summer until September.* By far the most important item of food on the trout's menu is the buzzer, which entomologists know as the chironomid and the most significant of these in April are the black species. During the early season the only other colours likely to be around in any quantity are the green and orange-silver. The sizes of the species differ from water to water and from year to year. Imitations dressed on size 10 or 12 hooks are probably the most versatile. Occasionally, very large buzzers are encountered and a hook size of 8 is desirable. (One could never forget those astonishing buz-

*See Appendix for details of the flies mentioned in the text

zers at Grafham in the early years.) More often smaller species will predominate, although it is rarely necessary to fish an imitation using a size smaller than a 14. Flies this small invite trouble, for to present them properly requires the use of very light leaders and allows the possibility of that ubiquitous devil – breaking on a fish. In the next chapter I consider more fully the use of fine leaders.

The most consistently successful fly for English still-waters I have ever found is the Pheasant Tail nymph, as recommended by Arthur Cove – tailless and with the dressing taken around the bend of the hook, buzzer fashion. It is a good general representation of several insects which are important to the trout, particularly buzzers and sedges, and, in smaller sizes, corixae and crustacea. In sizes ranging from 14 to 8, this is one of the finest flies a fisher can present for both brown and rainbow trout at all depths. There have been several seasons when I have been forced to change to other patterns of nymph purely because fishing the Pheasant Tail has become too easy. There can be no better accolade for a fly than that!

There is one other nymph that makes up my essential trio for the English stillwaters in spring. It was originally designed by Peter Grundel to imitate the large damselfly larva. Soon after early successes with this fly I adapted it for more general use. It goes under the rather unimaginative name of the Green nymph. On a visit to Orkney Peter had acquired a huge ball of the local wool in an unusual shade of green. We have never been able to find quite this shade elsewhere, although an exact copy of the colour is not necessary. It is pale and rather dull and the texture of this particular wool is fine. The Green nymph is one of those strange flies that at first glance looks unprepossessing. In fact it is extremely effective. In slightly coloured or weedy water, or when there are small buzzers about, the trout, particularly rainbows, accept it with

confidence, or, as Stuart puts it, they 'take it very per-
sonally'!

There are a few other nymphs which it is wise to have
for more occasional use. The orange-silver buzzer makes
its début towards the end of the spring. A sparse dressing
on a number 12 or 10 hook is best when these little
creatures are active. Olive and green buzzers are also often
abundant in the cold waters of spring. Large buzzer larvae,
known to fishers as bloodworm, are always about on the
lake bed at this time of year and trout will take red or claret
patterns, dressed thinly, in various sizes. Caddis, the
larvae of the dozen or so important species of sedge, also
abound by weed beds and on the lake floor, but there is no
better general pattern for these than the Pheasant Tail.

The last important fly for use at this time of year is the
hatching buzzer. When trout are right up in the surface
they are nearly always feeding on a hatch of chironomids.
On the point of eclosion a buzzer pupa releases carbon
dioxide between its adult body and the nymphal shuck
which is about to be discarded. At this time its abdomen
appears to be bright silver. My imitation of this stage of
the insect's life cycle is simple. I tie silver tinsel from the
bend of the hook (size 10 or 12) all the way up to the
thorax where I dub in some black wool, followed by white
wool or rabbit fur at the eye. Trout on the surface find this
pattern irresistible. Here we are approaching the traditional wet fly style, for this fly, and the method of fishing it, is
not dissimilar to working a lively Black Pennell on the top
dropper.

In concluding this discussion about early season flies I
should say that exact imitation is not only impossible but
unnecessary. Even if we could make a perfect copy of the
natural fly and then completely mimic its movements, we
would be largely wasting our time. With a thousand
naturals to choose from, why should a trout isolate our

copy? As Arthur Cove once explained, it is the imperfect imitation that will stand out and be noticed by the fish.

The biggest problem one has in the spring is that of finding trout. There can be long periods when there is no surface activity whatsoever and the lake looks empty. Local knowledge helps, though an ability to read the water cannot be beaten. The longer you spend observing still-waters under a wide variety of conditions, the more instinctive becomes the sense of watercraft. Eventually you will not have to think about where the trout might be, but will know more or less exactly where they are. Of course Nature has a way of humbling any man and, just when you think you perfectly understand a water system, so the trout disappear and are being caught elsewhere! The craft of fishing is about opening the senses to all the available information. The lakeside environment is a fascinating study in itself. With so much hidden beneath the waves, the fisher must work out what is happening in the depths with the aid of the fragments that can be observed.

The most difficult conditions occur when the wind blows hard from the east or north-east, the light is bright and the water clear and rather stark. Early in the year these conditions are often coincident. Such days are cold if not crisp and fly activity seems non-existent. On many days like this I have fished Bewl, Grafham and other stillwaters and have seen on the surface perhaps no more than half a dozen trout over very long periods. Leaping trout quicken the pulse, but usually they will be far off over the deep water with no pattern to their movements. Under these conditions the methods I use with the fly rarely work with any consistency. One has to toil and test the instincts to the limit, ignoring other fishers with fast-sinking lines. The cold east-wind days are the fly-fisher's nemesis. We wait for the wind to fall and the light to diffuse towards evening.

Fortunately these conditions do not last long. The longest I ever experienced them was at Bewl in 1984 when an easterly tore relentlessly across the lake throughout the last two weeks of April and the first week of May. In six visits I caught only six trout. Then came the westerlies and how the fish fed!

Settled weather is best and that usually means winds from southerly or westerly quarters. Even a north wind is reasonable, provided it is steady. The one which effectively douses the fly-fisher's spirits is a gale from the east.

I love lee shores or bays into which a wind is blowing, especially when the air is warm. Fly hatches can be sparse in the spring, but whatever insects there are will be blown where the wind takes them, and the trout will follow. There is a bay called Goose Creek on the southern arm of Bewl Bridge. Often a wind from north-west around to south-west blows into the creek. When this occurs for any length of time trout are usually present. If the wind blows out of the bay, or across its wide mouth, the area seems to be devoid of fish. I like to try well inside the Creek and at times it is as though every trout in Bewl is there. On several occasions I have taken a six-fish limit in half an hour from Goose Creek, but always when the waves are tumbling against its steep banks. Big, fast catches, however, are not what makes good fly-fishing. In 1985 I fished at Bewl on nearly twenty occasions and caught over a hundred trout, but what I consider to have been my best day passed as follows.

A north wind was blowing at about a force 3–4. It had been steady for a day or two so I made my way to the southern arm to find a lee shore. I walked along the bank looking for surface activity but the little I saw was well out over deeper water. I did not pause in Goose Creek, for the wind was cutting across its mouth. Passing by the woods north of the Creek one comes to a small bay that is rarely fished by bank anglers because to reach it requires a fair walk. Here I stopped. The wind was throwing a good swell against the beach.

Fishing into a breeze requires careful casting. Poor timing results in the line being curled back on itself. On a lee shore, however, trout are usually close to the bank, so long distances are not needed. It is the one occasion, other than when dry fly-fishing, that I prefer a short leader, say one of twelve feet. A single fly is called for as droppers can result in tangles when casting the necessary narrow loops.

There were a few buzzer shucks in the water. Without wading I punched out a small hackled buzzer and did no more retrieving than was required to gather in the loops of line that the wind was blowing towards me. After only a few casts the line tip shot away and I tightened into a good fish which unleashed some spectacular sub-marine whirls of motion, the line hissing as he sped across the bay, before I beached him, a 1½-lb brown trout. Of all the fish I caught at Bewl during that April and May only five were brownies. I was delighted; even more so when twenty minutes later the performance was repeated with another, this one being ¼ lb heavier than the first. At a time when few trout were being caught, the application of a little watercraft had made all the difference. All too often on our famous rainbow trout fisheries, anglers arrive and head straight off to where they have heard trout have recently been stocked or where good catches have been made. They anchor their boats above, or wade out towards, these shoals and cause mayhem among the often ill-conditioned fish. There has been no application of instinct and no investment into the warehouse of knowledge that makes a good fly-fisher.

Extensive areas of shallow water do not hold trout for very long in the spring, these areas being the summer grounds. It is better to find a place where deep water meets a shelf at a reasonable distance from the bank. Marauding shoals habitually sweep in from the lake on a feeding spree in such locations. Points and headlands or shelving bays are ideal. On Bewl, and also on Rutland, there are many of these. On Grafham there are fewer than there used to be because of the erosion. The north bay, the first big inlet on the north-eastern shore, used to be excellent water in the spring but, as the banks have collapsed now, and the trees are dangerously near one's backcast, it rarely fishes as well as in halcyon years.

One consequence of erosion is mud, which will be stirred up in rough weather. This is a mixed blessing for the fly-fisher. It can happen that a lee shore becomes totally unfishable because dense mud in suspension reduces visibility to a few inches. Trout are very unlikely to be in the thick clouds and even if they were there would be little chance of them seeing our flies. Sometimes, when bands of mud are stirred up, it is possible to cast beyond them. Not only will the lake bed be disturbed but also food items. Trout tend to hover or cruise just beyond the bands as they search for chance morsels. Provided we fish in the reasonably clear water with a bright fly – the Green nymph is perfect – the chances of a good catch are high.

In the colder months I avoid fishing with a wind coming directly from behind. The only good thing about a following breeze is that it is easy to shoot out a flatteringly long line. But no one could reach the far shore and it is there, in all probability, that most of the trout will be! Cold water from wintry depths is drawn up on to shores from which the wind is blowing and this suppresses insect activity. In addition, it is difficult to apply an attractive motion to the flies when the line lies more or less in front of the fly-fisher. An up and down movement is all that is possible, rather than the enormously effective drift and curve that is set up by a side-wind.

Therefore, the ideal place in a season's early months is a promontory jutting out into the lake, and one with a wind cutting across is best of all. A deepish bay with the swell coming in, though less comfortable, is also profitable.

In a flat calm, which is more likely to occur in the summer or in the late evening, these places are also good, but the fishing will be more demanding. Stealth is called for, and slow retrieves which cause a minimum of disturbance. It is all too easy to frighten off trout from calm water by careless wading and too-frequent casting. A long line is vital and it must be watched during the careful retrieve for any signs of movements. A tug, or simply the line behaving unexpectedly, might be caused by the fly catching in weed or the lake bed, but could just as easily be the result of a trout's unhurried take.

If a gentle breeze blows up in calm weather, little wavelets will appear in patches over the lake. If one casts to the edge of the ripple and allows small nymphs to drift slowly, patrolling trout, particularly rainbows, will often be found; although this method is verging on summer tactics which are the topic of the next chapter.

Storms whip up the spring waters, making for exciting fishing in the big waves. With the nymph anything greater than a force 5 makes presentation difficult. We are then back to the heavy fly and one with slightly more bulk than in any other conditions. I am convinced that one need *never* be tempted to use any hook longer than the international competition maximum (five-eighths of an inch), which is either a short shank 10 or 8, depending on the make. In pitching waters little flies are whipped around by the gale and trout will never see them. A heavy Pheasant Tail acts as a sort of sea-anchor, while fairly large nymphs or even traditional wet flies should be used on droppers. The Soldier Palmer, with its hackle wound up the body, is highly visible in a wild water. So too is a long-hackled

Black Pennell. I know several fishers who swear by a big Zulu in these conditions; but I hate the fly and have not used it for more than ten years. A wind from the side is best and the waves ought to be allowed to give the flies their movement. Any retrieve, until the line is lying virtually along the bank, will make them move too fast.

The calm lane is a curious phenomenon associated with windy, even wild, weather on large stillwaters. I have never heard a convincing explanation as to their origins, but I know that fishing a fly either in them or just by them is extraordinarily effective. Insects tend to be concentrated in these lanes of relatively calm water which can stretch for a mile or more across the lake. On stormy waters, calm lanes grow and shift. Wherever they approach a shore, a bank fisher will be able to reach trout.

I fished Bewl Straight one day in 1984 and the wind was strong, blowing along and slightly on to the eastern shore. A calm lane reached across the lake from Chingley Wood Point to a little Point on the bank where I was fishing. A

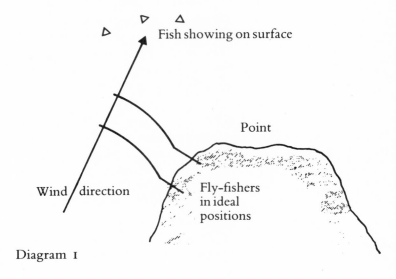

Diagram 1

boat was anchored about fifty yards offshore, though too far from the calm water. The two fishers in the boat had not touched a fish all day. The edge of the calm lane had brought three big rainbows to my net when, infuriatingly, the boat fishers decided to break the rules and moved to within twenty yards of me. Immediately they began to catch trout on lures that were probably named something like Death's Head or Mururoa Atoll! I moved on.

It is an insult to our sport that such bad manners are increasing on our fisheries. Finally they might merge with other modern ills to bring about the end, for when the gentle art gives way to mindless fishmongery it will be reduced to a base bloodsport, and I for one will say enough is enough.

My fly-fishing log has served to remind me of a rather significant tactic with respect to wind direction, and it involves one's position on a bank – or the guidance of a drifting boat. Again, some events over the last few seasons will help to illustrate the point.

Fishing from Old Hall Point on Rutland Water, there was a strong north-easterly blowing. Peter Grundel and I had noticed a few fish showing some distance offshore, well beyond casting range. Diagram 1 illustrates the situation. By extrapolating an imaginary line back from the showing fish along the direction of the wind we deduced the obvious place from which to cast. A 'drift' of water – one might see it as a river within the lake – was flowing in the direction of the arrow. This drift carried with it what insects there were that were active. Trout were attracted from the deep water a hundred yards or more from the Point and swam within range of the bank, only along the drift. Farther around the Point, which was superficially more attractive (other fishers had toiled away all day to no avail), the fishing was fruitless.

Exactly the same conditions have made excellent days for us, as distinct from ones that would otherwise have been difficult. Only last season at Bramble and Ferry Points at Bewl Bridge, steady winds set up these drifts and drew the fish in. One can be just a few yards too far away from water through which the trout are passing and, as Herbert Macdonald, ghillie on Loch Hope, is fond of saying: 'You might as well fish in the bath!' On days of sparse insect activity, at least, the trout simply will not leave the area where they are sure to find whatever feed is available. The trick is to cast perpendicular to these drifts, as shown in the diagram, and allow the wind to swing the flies quietly around. The trout might be fairly deep and not showing, but they are likely to be there, and feeding. On the above-mentioned day at Rutland the takes were coming to the tail nymph, at least ten feet down. Only later, in the evening, did the fish move at the dropper nymphs.

A rather more subtle wind and shore effect is illustrated in Diagram 2. This is also a fairly common situation. I believe that one of the best places to fish on Bewl Bridge is

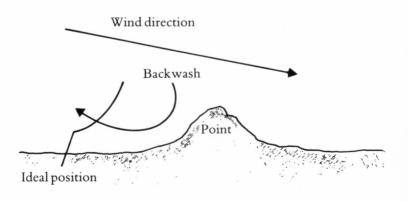

Diagram 2

1 Above: Sunset at Grafham, summer 1981

2 Below left: Stuart Broadhurst at Bewl Water, spring 1985

3 Below right: Brown trout ready for the net, Bewl Water, 1985

4–5 Above and below: Brown trout, Bewl Water, summer 1985

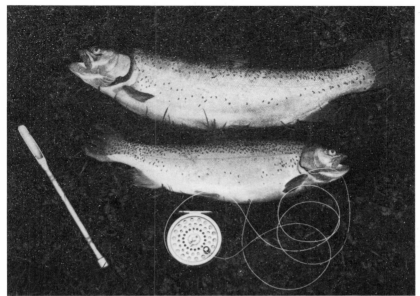

6 Above: Rainbow trout (6 lbs and $3\frac{1}{4}$ lbs), Bewl Water, summer 1986

7 Below: After the sport; winter on Bewl Water, 1985–6

8 Above: Loch Maree, c.1930 (courtesy of the Kinlochewe Hotel)

9 Below: Loch Maree from 1,200 feet, autumn 1980

when the phenomenon occurs of a slightly onshore wind blowing along that particular bank. Yet not one fisher in a hundred recognises its potential or bothers to pause for a few casts. The small Point seems on the surface relatively insignificant until one realises that, underwater, it continues as a marked feature of the lake floor and sets up a backwash or eddy in which nymphs and drowned flies are concentrated. One sees, in such locations, fishers heading directly for the Point itself, but so often it is far more productive to try upwind of this position, in the backwash, as shown. One should remember, however, that the backwash will disappear as soon as the wind blows slightly offshore.

Again, the above is a minor tactic which works with consistency, although it is just one of the many subtleties that the watchful fisher observes on a large stillwater.

I suppose that much of this can be classed as advice, and yet to me it is a pleasurable recounting of experiences by the lake shore. If I am consciously to offer any advice to fly-fishers faced with the challenge of bank-fishing our great waters, it must include all I have said about the light line cast a long way and the development of a sense of watercraft until it becomes instinct. Most of all, however, I would stress that the water is a friend, the wind an ally, the trout not merely objects to be trapped, but beautiful, mysterious creatures. To be thrilled by the bustle of life that shares our lakeland world is the key to a harmony we never lose. The good fly-fisher is not the one who, with thoughts only of satisfaction at having something more to add to the freezer, staggers early into the lodge with a limit of stock-fish when the season is but an hour old. The sportsman is he who still toils by the shore, fishing within limitations he has set himself, almost a part of the weather system, the water and the trout's mind, whether he has caught anything or not.

4

Long Days, Fair Winds

SOMETIMES IN MAY, sometimes as late as June, we discover that the air is no longer cold. Brown bracken and ochre grass on which we have trodden for two months has given way to lush, damp growth. The mud from April's downpours has dried and the ground is firm underfoot. The white of wood anemones has long since faded and even the bluebells are going over, purple rather than blue, on withering stems. Warblers chatter excitedly from behind fresh foliage; the lakeside is a lovely place in late spring and early summer.

The martins have arrived, with some swallows and swifts among them. The fork-tailed crescents weave the sky above calm waters as they, like the trout, feed on the hatch. They are friends to us fishers, for the place below their swooping flight is where our ever-hungry quarry lurks. A trout leaps, a swallow dives as buzzers breach the surface; and the fly-fisher is privileged to be there to see this subtle spectacle of summer.

The Points still fish well, for rainbows patrol wide areas in their search for feed and a fly-fisher can intercept them as they move from deeper water. There are places, however, other than promontories and lee shores, where we can now find the shoals. As the water warms so the trout become more dispersed. Large areas of shallows, in bays and on banks, are no longer scoured by cold winds, and in such places weed growth and insect life proliferates rapidly. Trout are attracted and many totally abandon their deep-water lies in favour of the bays.

One such place where it is good to be in the early summer is the Sanctuary Bank on the north-west shore of Grafham. This is a vast area of shallow water with a deeper channel cutting across it and running into Savages Creek. It is so shallow on the bank that in a prolonged drought (1976 was an example) one can wade out up to 400 yards beyond the place where we normally fish. In more usual conditions, along a mile and a half of shoreline, it is impossible to find depths of greater than six or seven feet at the limit of a long cast. There used to be 'hot spots' along Sanctuary where troughs ran from the deep close in to the bank. An old line of tree-stumps, which is still there, marked one of these, and a small Point another; but erosion has mainly levelled these and the bank is now more constant. None the less, it still continues to fish very well. Apart from the west bank, which is a nature reserve and does not open for fishing until mid-July, it is the wildest part of Grafham and it is possible to be alone there all day.

Fishing extensive shallows can be demanding. Only the largest shoals will be evenly distributed and, unless conditions have been steady and favourable for a week or more, there will be smaller groups of trout ranging the entire area. In restricted depth the fish often give themselves away by rising or jumping. It is best to look for places where surface activity is greatest, for one or two leapers might simply be passing through rather than feeding.

When Peter and I fished Sanctuary a few years ago we saw no evidence of trout activity anywhere along the shore. We knew that they had to be there because a soft, warm wind was blowing along the bank and a number of early mottled sedges were hatching off. We settled in a favoured spot a quarter of a mile east of Savages Point. In shallow water the exploration of all depths can be adequately accomplished with a two-fly cast. I tied up a size 10 Pheasant Tail on the point and Peter's design of Amber Sedge in a size 12 on a single dropper. We have used this latter fly at sedge time ever since Peter invented it in 1975. It is an excellent general representation of a sedge pupa and my friends and I must have taken hundreds of trout on this pattern. Along with the three flies mentioned in the preceding chapter it makes up the last of my four really essential nymphs for English stillwaters.*

Allowing the nymphs to drift in the wind, where they swept around two or three feet down – standard summer style in shallow water – we had exciting sport. We saw few fish on the surface until late evening. Unseen, the shoals were passing through, feeding on ascending sedge pupae without bothering with the flies hatching and skittering on the surface. We each had half a dozen splendidly conditioned trout. I also caught a 1½-lb roach which was a very handsome fish with his rich-red fins and delicate silver flanks. (Bream and roach are commonly caught on nymph at Grafham and many other stillwaters. In 1985, fishing this same area with Peter and Stuart, I was

* See end of chapter for dressing

lucky enough to catch another roach of about 2 lbs. This is the sort of fish of which coarse fishers dream, not particularly for any power the fish possesses but because 2 lbs is very heavy for the species and roach are a beautiful breed. Any coarse fish we catch we immediately return to the water. Peter, more than any of us, is accurate to within a few ounces of assessing a fish's weight.)

Summer is the time for exploring the lake shore. When the fair winds blow from the south and west fishing can become a simple task. Rainbow shoals, especially that particular season's stock which will be fish of between 1 and 2 lbs, are in prime condition and feed ravenously at this time, their richest opportunity in the entire year. Even if the fish have been quiet for most of the day, the evening rise, even a poor one, can nearly always be relied upon to bring the waiting fisher a burst of activity in the gathering dusk.

On larger stillwaters some fishers tend to walk a long way during the summer months, watching the water as they travel. Many have an interest in the environment in its entirety and spend much time observing the terns (which breed by both Bewl and Grafham) and other birds, or counting the different species of butterfly that abound along Grafham's north and west shores, or being a part of all those fascinating encounters with wild-life that add to the richness of our sport. Here and there we fish, by weed beds or on a bank that has an attractive breeze blowing along it; perhaps by a drowned tree-stump where a brown trout may lurk, or in a deep channel where huge rainbows have been splashing.

At this time of year I often fish just the one fly. There is a wide bay on the west shore of Grafham which is shallow and tends to be weedy in July and August. Nowadays it rarely holds a large number of trout; though on most afternoons three or four trout will be cruising around taking small fry, corixae or sedge. In quiet conditions such fish usually swim repetitively on the same curving course, with minor deviations. By observing them for a quarter of an hour one can almost set a watch by their movements. One has risen here, in half a minute he will show there . . . By carefully positioning oneself on the bank, these cruisers can be ambushed. Sometimes it is necessary to wade. At places like the west bank it is less than ten feet deep seventy yards offshore and the fish might be anywhere, cruising along the shallows, like patrolling submarines. Where there is thick weed it is best to wade towards the edge in order to keep the line as clear as possible. Then the fish might be a matter of feet from the bank. I can recall dozens of occasions when I have stupidly waded thirty yards out only to find trout rising happily behind me. Doesn't one feel a fool when that happens! Trout preoccupied with their feeding are often found hard up against the shore, in only inches of water. These fish are extraordinary sport. They are usually feeding on tiny fry or corixae, and the Pheasant Tail will take them, though a small silver-bodied nymph or wet fly can be better. Once hooked, the trout flay the water, carving the surface to foam. They shoot along like torpedoes, their tails lifting trails of stirred-up silt behind them. You can bet that they will rip off your entire fly line and the heavier fish will be well into the backing before you can turn them.

This sort of precise, highly visual sport is what makes summer fishing so thrilling. Perhaps it is best to leave the huge shoals to the boat fishers while the bank fisher concentrates on more individual prey along the shore. The battles become personal and varied. One fish may be caught in a hole among the weeds, another risen fifty yards off the bank as a shoal speeds past. The next may be a brown trout from the edge of the shelf. A hundred memories race across my mind's eye, but long gone are the years when I hammered the big shoals.

Peter loves silk-weed and in certain conditions so do I. After a long, hot spell with no rain, thick blankets of this filamentous algae bloom in shallow water. If you lift out a net full of this weed you will find all manner of insect and crustacean life, ranging from buzzers and dragon-fly larvae to snails and shrimps. Silk-weed is a trout's larder. It can also destroy a small lake which lies on fertile ground by the process of eutrophication, deoxygenation of the water; so it has to be controlled. As a point of interest, this process is the biochemical opposite of the infamous acidification. This latter evil, however, is virtually irreversible due to the leaching into the ecosystem of aluminium and heavy metal cations. Eutrophication, caused by nitrate and phosphate enrichment from agricultural waste and run-off, is highly destructive, but more easily reversed.

Both brown and rainbow trout patrol the channels and edges of silk-weed and they often shelter in the shade of rafts of the organism. In such places, we fish with one fly, often Pheasant Tails, though I am fond of the dry fly when the weed is up. Wading is necessary if growth extends far from the bank. Casting should be no more than a few yards beyond the bed. When fishing the nymph we use a style of 'sink and draw', allowing the fly to sink and then lifting it at various speeds towards the weed-rim. Two flies invite hooking up with strands of weed and this happens, now and then, even with one fly. Takes tend to be rather savage. Once a fish is hooked the problems begin because during the next five or ten minutes you have to steer a lively trout through highly obstructed areas of water. Obligingly, however, trout do not often run into the thicker regions of weed. Line of 6 lbs breaking strain is about right. Anything lighter leads to trouble because many of these trout will be heavier than the average and

45

during the fight the fly line is bound to pick up trailing and hanging strands of weed. The strain on the leader is considerable.

On July 15th 1981, Peter hooked a good trout at the edge of the weed. The fish fought deep for several minutes and broke the rules by running headlong into a thick bed. I was waiting at Peter's side with the landing net. One or the other of us said, 'Well, that's it, he'll leave the fly in that lot.' For another minute or so Peter put as much strain as he dared on the rod. Very slowly a huge clump of the algae rose to the surface. I turned to wade out while Peter hauled it in. 'Will you net it for me, the fly's buried in the middle of it?' he asked. This I did. The net was so heavy that I could not lift it from the water. We dragged it to the bank and together began to extract the leader. There in the middle of the green cloak was the most magnificent brown trout, the heaviest either of us had caught at Grafham for a number of years; a truly huge and perfect specimen. Peter loves silk-weed!

There is one more method which should be considered, for it is vastly underrated on stillwaters: the dry fly. Nearly every fisher one meets either secretly or openly believes there is something mystical about fishing the floating fly, doyen of the chalk streams. In fact it is a simple method. Fishing a nymph requires thought in three dimensions, an appreciation of the volume of water through which the fly travels. The two-dimensional plane of the surface is where the dry fly sits; one need not be concerned with depth. Summer trout spend long periods close to or on the surface. Even when feeding on the nymph they will rise to a hatched fly drying its wings in its new element. Matching the hatch is best, though in June, July and August there can be a dozen species simultaneously active on or near the surface. Fry-feeding trout are particularly susceptible to the dry fly. When trout are

46

being selective there can be no compromise; only a reasonable imitation will do. This occurs more in August than in any other month. I usually begin with my favourite size 12 Red Palmer and if that does not evoke a response I carefully try to assess what it is the risers are taking: this can sometimes be extraordinarily difficult.

Dry fly-fishing has the added virtue of being visually thrilling. Surely, one can never tire of seeing that glorious roll at the buzzer, the whirl at sedge or gentlemanly sip at sailing olives. The three families, diptera, trichoptera and ephemeroptera, are the most important insects for the stillwater fly-fisher. They are all of aquatic origin. The nymphs are certainly more important than the adult flies in as much as they are accessible over a longer period of time. The hatching sub-imago of all species, however, is highly attractive to trout, as also, but less so, is the spent, or egg-laying, imago. Feeding preoccupation is common on these surface-borne flies. Trout can also become pre-occupied by hatches and falls of other species, aquatic or terrestrial. I deal with the beloved crane-fly in the next chapter. During summer, however, we may come across dense hatches of ephemeroptera other than olives; for example, mayfly and caenis, hawthorn flies – or heather flies in moorland areas – red and black ants, beetles, moths and drone flies. In rugged, acid terrain, where nutrients are sparse, there are often several species of the hardy stoneflies.

Preoccupation only occurs during dense hatches or falls. Some wind-falls will bring about a weak response, or none at all. Those who knew Grafham during the drought years of the mid 1970s will remember the incredible hatches of ladybirds. Despite large numbers of these creatures finding their way into the water, friends and I did not find a single trout which had been feeding on the hapless insects. Hawthorn flies can bring about a slow response. If the falls continue over a reasonable duration trouts' interest increases.

Just as when nymph fishing, we attempt a vague imitation of the natural. The buzzers of spring have given way to different species, to brown and ginger, possibly the red, and often the large green. I successfully manage to imitate all species of dry buzzer with three patterns, in different sizes. On size 14, 12 and 10 hooks I dub either blank, emerald or amber wool. This I rib with lurex. The hackle is short and stiff in fibre, black, badger or red-game respectively. An added touch of grace is applied by tying in two white hackle tips, sloping backwards.

The Red Palmer I have already mentioned is a superb general representation of the many sedges that abound during high-summer. For closer imitation I add a wing of hen pheasant (from the wing or tail of the bird) cut into the characteristic roof-shape. I choose different coloured red-game hackles and pheasant feathers for the varied types of sedges we encounter. The basic Red Palmer, with its subtle gold rib, will usually work as well as anything else.

Wind-falls of terrestrial flies are more irregular than those mentioned above. We have to analyse the situation, sometimes very quickly. If the trout are moving at drones, say, in the surface we must have a reasonable imitation in the same place if we are to be successful. Patterns are important, although this book is not really concerned with fly dressing. I suggest, however, that the fisher be equipped with those flies mentioned above if he is serious about the imitative style on stillwater. The dressing is not as complicated as it sounds. In my experience a dozen patterns cover every eventuality.* By far the most important point is the method of fishing, as in all styles.

We are not concerned, as we are when fishing the

* See Appendix

nymph, with depth. We present our flies in areas of activity or potential. With falls of terrestrials it is usually best to fish where the wind is blowing off the land. Take care, however, and make careful observation – I can remember a number of occasions on highland lochs or wide arms of our southern stillwaters, when trout have moved on lee shores to terrestrial flies that have travelled right across the body of water.

I prefer to fish a single dry fly, lightly greased, rather than a combination of dry and nymph as favoured by many fishers. Yes, the dry fly can act as an indicator of a take to the nymph; but the smooth glide of leader and line is better. I often fish across the wind, casting as much into the wind as possible. It is very like fishing the up-stream dry, your offering drifting back towards you and then off, down-drift. Occasionally, feeding trout prefer an imitation in, rather than on, the surface, fished as a hatching nymph. Sedges are the only flies that I sometimes retrieve fairly quickly, when the fish are in the mood for a chase.

A twelve-foot leader is usually adequate. One has to avoid the leader curling back over the fly line on delivery. There is no doubt that a tapered leader is ideal, especially when casting into the wind. Presenting into strong winds will require short, steeply tapered leaders. Such 'storm-casts' can be equally useful when fishing nymph on lee shores.

I never grease the leader anywhere near the fly. This ensures a minimum of surface disturbance. A good rub-down of the nylon with mud or detergent is best.

Just when I believe that I adequately understand a water, something happens which is very good for me: August. All through the season I might have been happy with my progress on the big lakes and then a day invariably arrives when my over-inflated ego is shattered and I walk the banks a frustrated mass of jangling nerves. It nearly always happens in that dreaded month and it may happen two or three times in one season. There was an occasion on Grafham in 1975 when a good wind was blowing, there was a fair light and trout were everywhere. All day long, from the moment Jim Mitchell and I arrived until the late evening, there was barely a time when we did not see several fish splashing about in the water. I tried everything I knew. After a few hours without the slightest indication of a take I believed in nothing except my incompetence. Here were feeding trout that must have seen a dozen of my flies, fished by a dozen styles, all of which were totally ignored. After six hours, quite by chance, I landed a small Mallard and Claret exactly where a trout rose. I had virtually put the fly into its mouth. At last I had a fish. It was crammed with tiny black, olive and green buzzers. I persisted with the Mallard and Claret to no avail, then tried a team of small buzzers, again without success; in fact neither Jim nor I had another take all day. I later received some sort of consolation when I discovered that two well-known but loud-mouthed 'experts' had also been fishing at Grafham that day and had returned in the evening without a trout between them. 'Must have had twenty takes,' one of them was heard to shout, 'but the bloody things came short.' That, really, said it all.

Often in high summer during warm weather, daphnia swarm in our stillwaters. Rainbow trout feed on these clouds of plankton much as baleen whales sift krill from the sea. This food form is one of the few that can force rainbows very deep. In bright conditions the daphnia swim into the depths, even below forty feet. Under more normal conditions, with the daphnia not far below the surface, Arthur Cove recommends the use of an orange nymph, fished fairly fast. This technique is often deadly to trout. But invariably there are a few days in August when all my efforts are virtually fruitless. I take refuge, however, in the fact that I have never met a fisher using fly-only methods who can honestly say that he too has not been bewildered in the heat of August; although this is all part of the fascination of trout – their ways, or not, with a fly.

One answer to the problems we have during these sultry days when, perhaps, trout become preoccupied with small food forms, is to fish fine leaders, as much to present tiny imitations correctly as to avoid frightening wary fish with monofilament that is too thick. We can, as I have said, easily break on a trout when using fine leaders, although there are several ways of avoiding this. The wrong knot can drastically reduce breaking strain and make a leader less resilient to sudden shocks. In my experience, and that of most of my companions by the water, the popular blood-knot is relatively poor. I use it only for joining the false butt to the leader, for which purpose it is reasonably safe. The traditionally weak points of a cast are the dropper knots. Here I *never* tie the blood-knot, at least since various disasters resulting from its use in the early 1970s. The three- or four-turn water-knot, however, using the down-pointing trailing end, is the best form of attachment I have yet found. The last weak point is the knot which joins fly to cast. Again, I dislike the most popular knot for this connection, which is the half-blood, even the 'tucked' form. My choice here is a two-turn turle-knot which, besides its utter reliability, has the advantage of never allowing a fly to twist sideways-on to the leader.

There is an elastic material now available that effectively absorbs much of the shock when a trout takes a fly at speed. A few inches of this product between false butt and leader is adequate to avoid the event of a 'smash' take. Thereafter, even the clumsy handling of a lively fish should not result in a break. As a point of conjecture, however, I believe we should not really need such a material if we are correctly retrieving and tightening into a trout. There are many 'gadgets' in fly-fishing, as in any other sport, designed to make the end-result more easily achieved. It seems to me that the goal should rather be to achieve a state of perfection with a minimum of equipment. I suppose braided leaders fall into the 'gadget' category; but they are good shock absorbers and marvellous extensions to fly lines.

The angle at which the rod is held with respect to the line of the flies' motion is important. With the rod pointed directly at the flies, which is common, nowadays, when nymph fishing by feel rather than sight, the shock of a take is transmitted directly to the hand holding the line. Again, with fine leaders, this often causes a break. It is better if the rod is held so that a bow of line falls from rod-tip to water surface, or that the rod makes an angle of about 130° with the fly line. In this way the rod and line can fulfil their function of absorbing sudden impacts. I have summarised these points in Diagram 3.

Another detail in this context is the choice of hook on which to dress the fly. Although tempting for small flies, it is ridiculous to use hooks formed from fine wire for large brown or rainbow trout (and even more so for sea-trout for which we often have to fish with fine leaders and small flies in calm weather). I have never found such a hook that does not bend or break with reasonable finger pressure. How well I remember an evening at Grafham when the sedge were up. The water surface was flat and the only movements were caused by the struggling insects, and marauding trout flashing through the shallows. I was using some sedge pupae dressed on fine wire hooks. They seemed perfect for the job, hanging, because of the fine wire, just below the surface. I had three takes in as

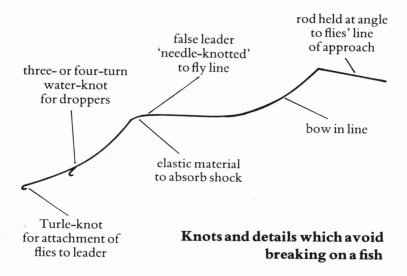

rod held at angle
to flies' line
of approach

false leader
'needle-knotted'
to fly line

three- or four-turn
water-knot
for droppers

bow in line

elastic material
to absorb shock

Turle-knot
for attachment of
flies to leader

**Knots and details which avoid
breaking on a fish**

Diagram 3

many casts and lost all three fish as I tightened. In each case
the hook had either opened at the bend or broken off
behind the barb. Furthermore I am certain that all three of
the trout were rainbows in excess of 3 lbs, while the last
one was in the region of 5 lbs. The company that had
produced these hooks was not very popular on the north
bank of Grafham that evening!

That event took place more than ten years ago. One
might expect, along with the development of other fine
equipment available to the modern fly-fisher, that hooks
are always reliable nowadays. This is *not* the case. The
hooks I use are as follows: Mustad Viking 94836A, a
splendid, forged, bronzed hook with a short point and
small barb; Mustad Viking 94840, a heavier version of the
above hook, with a longer point – I file the points right

down and use this hook for heavier nymph patterns that I want to fish near the lake bed, or for wet flies in stormy weather. The relatively new Captain Hamilton range of Partridge hooks is superb. From this one range you can choose the specific hook for the fly. The medium-weight wet fly and standard dry fly hooks are as close to perfection as a hook can be, with just the right gape for each respective shank. For more variation in ballasting, there is an International series, produced in three thicknesses of wire, in the same range. These hooks are also useful for some fly needs, though the gapes are slightly too great for others. There are other good makes of hook; but there are also some awful ones which should be banned. One should always test a sample hook from a pack by clamping it in the vice and twisting and flicking it. If it is held in the vice only by the point and it does not break, or open under reasonable pressure, then the other hooks in that pack should be reliable. I have never been let down by any of the hooks listed above.

Once instinct is primed and fundamental necessities are developed, both of which take only a love of the sport and much practice, there is nothing particularly difficult – other than those odd days I have mentioned – in trout fly-fishing. Some of the pillars of our establishment have a nasty habit of trying to convince us that they know best and that it is incredible that any of us lesser mortals ever catch fish. They are the self-appointed guiding influences of the sport who claim to be improving our techniques and they are reaping financial rewards in doing so. But so much nonsense is spoken and so much pseudo-science has crept up in order to support high-sounding theories. I have seen and fished with a good number of this mildly irritating breed of men; but I have shared the company of only four, possibly five, true masters, and I say this after over twenty years of concentrated activity on some of our most famous stillwaters. To mention names would be puerile and I refuse to play that game. I merely offer as a warning to those fishers who seek happiness through the art of rod, line and fly that they should not be brow-beaten into accepting the doctrine of every apparent expert. The only strength that leads to any lasting success is one's own. The advice in this book is gathered from experience and I am sure that what has worked for me under certain conditions may well fail for the next man, for can anyone fully understand even another human being, let alone another animal? And there is bound to be another fisher who knows something I do not about a water we both fish. Indeed there are only two places in the world where I would happily take on all-comers – both are sea-trout lochs in the north-west – simply because through long association I have come to know nearly every significant feature they contain.

Fly-fishing is not a competition with other men. The only competitors are you and the trout. And if you return unharmed the prize you have trapped, then you have both won.

5

Cool Mists and
Quick Storms

THE WEATHER IN this country, being what it is, can break
down overnight to ravage the countryside with a squall
from the west, only to clear again by dawn when the
fly-fisher finds motionless, clear airs above the silent lakes.

At the end of August we move into the last phase of
trout fishing which continues into the final, failing days of
October. The fish are at their most fascinating at this time
of year. They rest for long periods in places which
summer has taught them are safe holts, and then they
sweep into favoured feeding grounds where they gorge
themselves in preparation for the lean winter months
ahead. The spawning urge, at its peak in November,
forces them to feed in order to collect a stock-pile of
energy to sustain them. By and large shoals contain fewer
fish, though it is mainly the heavyweights that remain.
Dispersal is at its greatest in September, when trout will be
found on much of the good holding water. After sum-

mer's heat-waves, which drove the shoals into deeper, cooler water during August, autumn rains refresh the surface.

Slowly the leaves are mellowing, weed beds are shrinking and the sun's heat on the fisher's neck is less intense. During high summer our best chances have been at dawn when we may have been lucky enough to surprise a few trout in shallow water before they sneaked off to spend the day in the shaded deep. Now the sun crests pink above fairy mists which cling to dew-glistened grass. A wet wind springs and trout whirl in the bays as big buzzers – absent for the past two months – return, and corixae and snails take on their mini-migrations. Stillwaters are never still. Even during the dog days of August there is the perpetual motion of flies and fingering currents and convection thermals. In September, life quickens until silence returns at dusk as pockets of mist creep back over the water.

The fisher, his senses sharpened by summer's challenges, is at his best at this time of year; but so are the trout, for the survivors are the ones that make few mistakes. The persistent hunter has miles of bank space to himself now that the days are cooler. There are also more variations in fly pattern and presentation than during either of the two other phases of the year.

Sedges are still around, though hatches become more erratic, and buzzers proliferate as autumn progresses, much as they did in the spring. Often these two flies hatch simultaneously. When this occurs it is almost a rule of thumb that the trout, especially the heavier fish, will take the buzzers. I do not know why this should be so, but there might be dozens of mottled sedges lifting away from the surface and only a few chironomids, yet a trout will have a buzzer imitation every time. The pupae of sedges are rather more active than those of chironomids and it may be that the latter are simply an easier prey for the trout, requiring less expenditure of energy.

Snails have a peculiar means of travelling from one part of a lake to another. Abandoning the weed stems, they float upside-down, their mucous-coated feet clinging to the surface. There they travel at the wind's whim across the lake's depths until they reach fresh pastures in some distant shallows. These migrations can be on a massive scale and always occur in calm conditions when there is no more than a slight breeze. Trout then become like whales again, cruising along the surface, mouths casually opening and closing on the glut of little creatures which are quite unable to escape. The fish become totally preoccupied with this food form and they are not easy to catch. The problem is that they tend to be non-directional as they travel, turning this way and that, apparently at random. They will only take an imitation that is in the surface film. One that sinks or floats too high is usually ignored. Only a reasonable imitation of this crustacean is required. A Black and Peacock Spider is as good as any. Some fishers incorporate a buoyant material – Ethafoam or cork – under the dressing. I prefer to tie a bulky body of black wool and peacock herl as described in the Appendix. If only the hackle is greased one can be sure that the fly will float in the right place. Next a trout has to see it. While wallowing or cruising on or near the surface, a fish's field of view is essentially restricted by the mirror plane above him. He will not see a fly trapped in the film a few feet away. I have heard of fishers using three snail patterns on one leader only to suffer the ignomy of trout refusing all three. I have had Black and Peacock Spiders totally ignored by trout barely inches away. The rise to snail is slow and unhurried and can last all day and into the night. Fish do not need to expend more energy than is necessary to allow them to cruise casually on the surface. Sooner or later you will land a snail imitation in a trout's path. He will have it with a gentle sip, or up-and-over roll, and there will be chaos when he takes flight. It is exciting sport for, like so much in September and October, it is highly visual. One can be on first-name terms with the trout before he has even seen your fly! Snails are taken by trout in wilder weather, either from migrants caught out by a storm, or the sedentary creatures on fronds of weed. If you catch a fish with a rock-hard belly that grates as you press it, that is a sure sign of snail feeding. Any dark pattern of wet fly fished very slowly should be effective.

In the cool airs and sudden gusts of wind that typify autumn, falls of both terrestrial and aquatic insects regularly occur. During the warmth of the day, fly activity is high, but as the freshness of dew-point approaches in the evening so the insect's mating dances are doused and they fall, spent, on to the water. A billion microscopic eggs sink unseen to the lake bed where they will recolonise and replenish the fatigued mud while, above, the adults lie dying, to be mopped up by opportunistic trout. Matching with an artificial fly the general size and colour of the insects in the fall can be important; particularly one very special windfall, the crane-fly or, as it is more commonly known, the daddy-long-legs.

I am very fond of these gangly-limbed creatures which abound in September. In fact they have saved many an August day for me as well. They are a terrestrial insect which eclode from their pupae known as leather-jackets, which live in damp grass and bracken. They are cumbersome in flight and even a gentle breeze sweeps many out over the water where they fall. They make barely a movement as they lie with their long trailing legs on the surface, easy victims to the trout.

I first discovered the power of these flies as fish-takers in Scotland, on the hill lochs and then the big sea-trout lochs,

59

where I either dapped them or fished them dry on a long line. Provided that an imitation is of comparable size to the natural flies – it should certainly be no larger – and has incorporated in the dressing six trailing legs (the number is unimportant, for I am sure that trout cannot count) made from knotted strands of cock pheasant tail, it will attract fish. It is best also if the hackle is sparse and stiff, allowing the fly to sit on rather than in the surface. Being fairly large this fly is highly visible in the gloaming and one can fish it into the late evening. It hypnotises the fisher as it sits out there on the crimson-tinted waters of dusk. Soon a pair of jaws looms out of the darkness and the fly is gone. Nearly always the trout will be far larger than the average in the lake and if you hook him there will be no time for another cast. He fights in the darkness and leaps far out from the shore. He shatters the peace of night and you see him fifty yards away, a dark crescent against the last streaks of light in the western sky. At last you net him and tranquillity returns to the lake. Against the rest of the day's catch he looks huge. A dew in the air and scents from shore and water merge with the bitter-sweet smell of trout. Cold spring and summer's heavy heat are barely remembered, for autumnal paradise diminishes all else.

The fry which were tiny silver needles in early summer are now between one and three inches in length and some large trout become preoccupied with them in September. Lure fishers have good sport at this time; but the fly-fisher has a problem. In June and July, when fry are small, a Pheasant Tail or Green nymph, or perhaps a bright traditional wet fly, is highly effective in taking fry feeders. In September our flies are hopelessly undersized. But there is a method which is peculiarly successful. It stems from the way in which trout feed on fry.

Now and then a hunting trout cuts into a shoal of

sticklebacks or young perch, roach or bream and snaps up a single fish, cleanly extracted from the mass. I believe that this type of fry feeding is not the most common. Much more frequently a trout will use his bulk and speed, thrashing through the shoal to kill or stun the fry. Soon he turns back to take his helpless victims at his leisure. And here is the key to the fisher's line of attack. The stunned fish either sink to the lake bed or float and writhe at the surface. Anyone who has seen these hapless creatures will have noticed how pale they are. A white or cream dry fly, dressed on a size 8 or 10 hook and cast among disturbed fry, can prove fatal to marauding trout. Against bright skies an object on the surface is seen by the trout in silhouette. A dark, red-game pattern of dry fly seems even more effective than white flies in bright conditions. On some occasions the fly ought to be moved, fairly slowly and erratically, in imitation of an injured fish. Another day will demand that the fly be left motionless. One has to experiment, although there is plenty of time for this as our quarry can spend all day feeding on nothing but fry.

I fish less than I used to in the south of England during the autumn. The sea-trout lochs of the north-west have far too strong a pull, and there is so little time available that a fly-fisher must pursue the methods which give him the greatest emotional reward, in the places he loves best. All too soon the frosts have set their decelerating influence upon the lakes and the days have shortened. The trout, the thousands of survivors of our clumsy efforts, lie in peace. And we have had seven glorious months full of memories to add to the stock-pile of special images that our sport collects. The lakes of England – even the man-cultured ones – have been pools of excitement and learning, for I can think of no other human activity that has combined so harmoniously with nature to produce environments so rich and varied as Grafham, Rutland or Bewl Bridge, or the hundreds of other stillwaters that lie in our beautiful countryside. They are resounding examples of what can be done to benefit both man and wildlife. Among the heaped wreckage elsewhere the lakes give a sense of hope and optimism.

We have misused our great stillwaters. I tell people time and time again that Grafham is one of the most important fisheries in England. When it opened it heralded the explosion of interest in lure techniques. So too did it bring to the South Midlands a water reminiscent of the large lochs and loughs of Scotland and Ireland where we could practise traditional fly methods. With other large still-waters, Grafham continues to be a magnificent fishery, even as it is assaulted by methods on the edge of the rules. Rid of these methods, I am certain that it would be better. The Anglian Water Authority have offered the fishing lease for sale. I pray that the right management, one with vision, takes over. If we lose Grafham we will lose the English roots in certain stillwater techniques. If we lose Rutland also, perhaps as a mixed fishery, with a total abandonment of fly-only rules (it has been suggested), then could Bewl and Blagdon hold on? Could any of them?

Part Two

Wild Waters

6

Into the Hills

Fʀᴇsʜ ꜰʀᴏᴍ ᴛʜᴇ ʟᴀᴋᴇs of England, with their fat
rainbows, one has to adjust to the fisheries of the north.
The climate and scenery, the fish and the character of the
water, are all so different. Forgotten now are the bluebell
woods and soft, agricultural land, gentle hills and alkaline
acreages. We are in wild country, the wildest still remaining in Europe, along with the high alps and the fjords of
Scandinavia. West and north Norway must come closest
in terms of dramatic country, with breathtaking mountains and high cliffs cutting up from deep coastal waters.
But then it is facile to compare terrains. It is enough that
such undeniably majestic areas do exist.

We pass through scenery of dramatic change, from
mountains to high moor, through forests to winding
expanses of glacier-formed lochs. The shattered, furious
coastline totals not hundreds but thousands of miles as it
winds and claws around islands and sea lochs and massive

promontories jutting into the western approaches and the north Atlantic. U-boats hid off this coast as they sought prey among the convoys, the Vikings raided for three centuries, never exhausting the possibilities of fresh hunting grounds, while the Romans never dared explore among these ferocious seas and the war-like inhabitants of the northern lands. This shoreline and the sprawling mountains of the interior have thus far protected north-western Scotland from the irreversible damage that has been wrought elsewhere. Changes have occurred, especially in the removal of vast tracts of the ancient Caledonian forest, but the land remains startlingly beautiful.

The Highlands and islands quite overwhelm me. My heart lies there and when away, even on Grafham's long banks, I feel incomplete and restless. A man possessed only of slight emotion cannot be unimpressed by this landscape, with its lochs, legends, history, rapidly changing weather, and the sea, everywhere the turbulent sea. The trout fisher is in paradise in Scotland, north, west or south-west of Inverness.

I first visited Scotland as a small boy and the memories from that time have made me insatiable. Now, as often as possible, I take the long roads leading up to and filtering out beyond the Highland Line.

The fly-fisher must also adjust to his quarry, which is a very different animal from that found in southern waters. Essentially we are dealing with the brown trout and the sea-trout. The only other species that concerns us is the salmon and, occasionally, char. These fish present us with a wider spectrum of sizes than we find on English still-waters where, mostly, we catch trout of between 1 and 2 lbs in weight. When, for example, I have bothered to work out the average weight of trout that I have caught in a season from Grafham, I have found it to be in the region of 2 lbs in recent years. On some hill lochs which I fish regularly the average is ½ lb, on others it is 1 lb and on one or two as much as 1½ lbs. The sea-trout lochs, of course, tend the other way, where the run-of-the-mill fish is comparable, in terms of weight, to the Grafham mean; but a week's catch might include some very heavy sea-trout and salmon which makes an average have no meaning.

The whole flavour of the sport, however, is different from that found elsewhere. For me the only common thread is that I use the same tackle as in the south, light rods and lines that have given such faithful service; whether it be for fun with half-pounders in the hills or energy-sapping marathons with sea-trout and salmon.

It is difficult for me to know where to begin. Memories jostle one another and my mind's eye flickers from one rise of a brown trout to the leaping fury of a fresh-run salmon and, ultimately, to the unbelievable power of a heavy sea-trout. Perhaps it will be best to start where I began my own exploration of Scotland, in the hills and heather by the shores of lonely lochs and lochans. I must, however, introduce an attitude which might only have been hinted at until now.

Given that the Highlands have survived as long and as much as they have, despite human interference, it is certain that an area so fragile, notwithstanding its size, will eventually give way under ceaseless exploitation. The Atlantic salmon is now relatively scarce in its wild state. Even on some of the most famous of our sea-trout fisheries – Maree, Hope, Stack, Eilt, Shiel – the migratory trout is not nearly as plentiful as it was two decades ago. Possibly the brown trout is alone in surviving in comparable numbers to those found in our fathers' days. The blame for the depletion of natural fish stocks lies with various activities, all of them human. The fly-fisher is part of the equation, no matter how small a fraction, that eventually leads to the simultaneous answers: destruction and extinction. When drifting those huge lochs we might take a few sea-trout and return at dusk in the knowledge that there are many, many more left in the water, unharmed. But migratory fish on a run into freshwater are there for the purpose of breeding. Interference with that process, multiplied time after time, season after season, on noted fisheries, is bound to affect the system. On Loch Maree, for example, was it the nets, or UDN (Ulcerative Dermal Necrosis), that savagely reduced the stocks of heavy sea-trout? Or was it the enormous catches made by fly-fishers in the years up to the late 1960s? Common sense suggests that each of these is partially to blame.

Through long acquaintance with the northern lochs I have become convinced that fly-fishers can do rather more damage than we are prepared to admit. I know that it is incomparable with commercial fishing in the sea and estuaries, with the big business of poaching and the pollutants of acid rain and agricultural waste. None the less it is a significant factor and it is growing. In the man-maintained fisheries of parts of England and lowland Scotland, there is no problem other than the expense of restocking and water management. A wild fishery, however, must be preserved as such. Farming an indigenous stock might, at considerable expense, ensure survival of the loch. At the time of writing, a small-scale experiment of this type is being carried out on the Ailort/Eilt system. This involves the rearing of sea-trout in cages close to the estuary of the Ailort. When the trout have reached about 2 lbs in weight they are either released into the sea or transferred directly to Loch Eilt. The early results of this experiment seem to be encouraging in the short term; but we are on dangerous ground, for with too much human interference a natural system ceases to be truly wild and we have lost something very precious.

It is probably far better to limit the pressures in the first place, and this applies as equally to the hill lochs as to the sea-trout waters. There is nothing clever in the killing, but some flaw in man seems to need a heavy creel to demonstrate his skill. Deep down we know what we are doing and, no matter what others think, the inner man is the only true judge.

The road north from Lairg to Altnaharra passes the black shores of Loch Shin and then continues up on to the moor with its awesome landscape, festooned with lochs, which stretches in every direction farther than the eye can see. The single-track road snakes on and on while we begin to realise the tremendous size of Sutherland, the most north-western county of mainland Britain. Beyond the Crask Inn one passes through Strath Vagastie and at last the little hamlet of Altnaharra appears, nestling in the mountains at the head of Loch Naver. Here we are in the heart of some of the world's finest game fishing. If one were to stay a lifetime at Altnaharra, or any of the dozens of other fly-fishing centres in Sutherland or Ross, all the possibilities of surrounding lochs could not adequately be explored. The village is a crossroads at which the fly-fisher is in a dilemma to know which way to turn. Running eastwards the road passes Loch Naver before curving north-east along Strath Naver, following this prolific salmon river almost all the way to the coast at Torrisdale Bay. Northwards lies Loch Loyal, the road rising above Loch Craggie and finally sloping down to the sea at the Kyle of Tongue. West of Altnaharra a track, rather than a road, passes through the spectacularly rugged country of Strath More towards Loch Hope, the most northerly large sea-trout loch on the mainland. No matter which road you take you will see stillwaters at every turn, some huge, others tiny, though nearly all of them contain trout which make it worthwhile to pause. Regardless of which direction you take in this lovely country you will be bound to find a plethora of lochs in the hills.

Unlike England, where fly-fishing can be expensive, brown trout in Scotland belong to the common man – by law. Protected by this constitution, a fly-fisher might believe he is within his rights to try for trout wherever he pleases, for there is also no law of trespass in the north. This having been said, there are several complications, and also we are in fly-only country where it is always best to seek the sanction of estate owners to fish the lochs which lie on their land. There may, after all, be a grouse shoot on the day you intend to fish. Having been too close for comfort to some of those marksmen of questionable talent (and eyesight), I have no desire to repeat the performance. An owner may have any number of reasons for suggesting you stay off certain parts of his land, but only on a few occasions have I met with an antagonistic response. On land entirely under estate care an owner will usually be only too pleased to have you fish his lochs; they might not have been fished for seasons. He might even allow you to use his boats if he has any. Estates, however, are not what they used to be. All too often nowadays the smaller ones tend to be resorts for the wealthy and the houses are closed down for most of the year. Official sanction then cannot be obtained, but you are fully entitled to go ahead and fish, provided you do no damage to any property.

Much of the hill fishing is run by the hotels on some sort of loose rota basis. Of course, the lochs are open to non-residents. Also permits are usually obtainable from village post offices and general stores, and a small fee is charged. This is ostensibly used to maintain the lochs and any boats kept on the larger ones. The fees are low on all but a few prized lochs run by mercenary hoteliers.

I once had the following conversation with one of these

fellows. He had just handed me a bill for a few days' stay
and I had noticed, with some horror, the figure £42 under
the title 'fishing' on a scrawled section of this piece of
ruinous paper.

'O.K.,' I began, as politely as I could, 'but what's this
amount for the fishing? Surely that can't be right?'

With an air of some surprise he took back the piece of
paper and scanned the account. 'Yes, that is all in order,'
he announced, glancing up to see me fuming. 'A day on
Craggie, another on Loyal and then two on the Skerray
chain.' He looked up at me as wide eyed as a rabbit. How
could I possibly question this nouveau-laird of loch
fishing?

'But I only visited the Skerray lochs on one of the days I
had booked for. You know that.'

'Ah yes,' he replied gathering himself for what he
thought was the *coup de grâce*, 'but I had to charge you for
the boat on both the days.'

'Have you been up to Skerray lately?' I asked.

'Not in a wee while, no.'

I knew that it was highly unlikely that he had ever seen
these lochs. 'Because if you had you would know that the
boat is unusable and I shouldn't think it has been taken out
for five years.'

'Well,' he exclaimed, 'perhaps it takes on a bit of
water . . .'

'No, not a bit. At the moment it's lying with half its hull
ripped out in four feet of water, on the bottom. I know, I
caught a trout right by it!'

He adjusted the bill. This Highland buccaneer is no
longer at that particular hotel. Doubtless he has moved on
to seek more accommodating custom.

Generally speaking, however, my encounters with the
characters of the north-west have been, in their own way,
as rewarding as the fishing, for that special land breeds

some extraordinary people and many strange stories spanning the spectrum from humour to sadness.

Ten years ago I lost count of all the lochs I have fished. I suppose I might have fished two that were almost identical but if so I cannot remember the pair. There are, however, basic themes which link some of them. Rift-valley lochs, caused by movement in the earth's mantle, are massive and deep. Ness is an example. They always contain trout, but the fish might be highly localised, close to the shore, or on sub-marine reefs and shallows produced over thousands of years of silt deposition at the mouths and deltas of rivers that flow into them. Another type, glacier-formed lochs, are common throughout the Highlands. Carved in ice-ages by colossal movements of ice-sheets, these lochs also tend to be large, but are usually more characterful than the rift-valley waters. Maree must be the premier example, festooned with islands, bays and points and strewn with boulders and shallows, despite some extremely deep water.

Lava-bed lochs are the most numerous of all and it is these that the fly-fisher finds in the hills. They are also variable in character. Formed by ancient volcanic activity and subsequent moulding in the last ice-age, they are invariably relatively shallow depressions, rarely exceeding forty or fifty feet at their maximum depth. The best of these, in terms of the weight of trout they contain, occur in limestone belts. Sometimes a loch or lochan might appear to be lying only on hard rock in acid moorland, but springs from deep layers of alkaline rock often flow into them. These waters always possess a stock of heavy trout. With no such enrichment, lochs on open moorland can become too acidic to contain anything more than very small fish. I know of one loch above Torrisdale Bay where the water is blacker than peat and as acid as I have found anywhere. It is in a bowl of boggy terrain. I am convinced that there are no trout in it whatsoever. Yet all around this loch, on slightly higher ground, are others where the fishing is first class. Some far-sighted estate owners, keepers and angling concerns have in the past done much work in tending over-acid lochs by adding phosphate and nitrate fertilisers and then carefully tending the weed and trout population. Sadly this practice is dwindling, though it still occurs in some areas, and the moorland is reclaiming many fine lochs in its acid grip.

I have said that the banks of the larger English lakes can be daunting; but they pale into insignificance against the sheer volume of fishing in the north. First one has to isolate an area; Altnaharra, Forsinard, Kinlochewe, Gairloch, Lairg, Durness, to mention but a few. This is a personal matter and takes into account one's taste in highly varied scenery. Fitness is a major factor, for hundreds of lochs lie several miles from the nearest path and one must toil over rough country to reach them. We must remember that we are in wilderness, the domain of eagles and nomadic deer, and we civilised creatures must take care in our venture. Perhaps it is best to be with others as we head into the hills. Certainly it is safer; although to be alone on the high moor is a spiritual and emotional experience. Only the memory remains when we return to the human order of things, but even those fleetingly remembered images are special. We flirt with a cruel history as we pass by the relics of ancient brocs and deserted crofts, and higher up, among the mountains themselves, we pause, where Viking expeditionaries may have done, to rest our weary limbs and feast our eyes on panoramas that shock our sophisticated minds.

When alone in the hills, until one is sure of the route and knows the country well, it is essential to have an Ordnance map and a compass, and to know how to use them. So too must we keenly watch the weather. Even in June or July the conditions can change with alarming rapidity. I have often been caught in violent storms or, worse, in sudden falls of mists and clouds. One totally loses all sense of spacial awareness in the mist's grey void. It is terrifying to be trapped in a deserted landscape and not to be able to see more than a few feet in any direction. Some say you should have plenty of food with you when in the hills and that it is best to sit-out the mist; but I can hardly recommend that. These conditions can persist for days – and nights! It is always wise to tell someone where you plan to go for the day; family, friends, hotel staff. Then, if you are missed, a search can be organised. I am a coward nowadays in unfamiliar territory. When I was younger I used to fish high in the hills while clouds wrapped themselves ominously around me. Now I would far rather be certain of living to fish another day. At the sign of lowering clouds I bolt for home. One day, I fear, I will sprain an ankle or break a leg, and then I shall just have to hope that someone loves me enough to come and fetch me from my folly.

In my youth an old ghillie once told me that if I was caught out by the mist I should walk until I found a burn and then follow that down. 'Always move downhill,' he advised.

'But what if the burn leads to a loch?' I asked.

'Then find a burn which flows out of it and follow that.'

'And if I can't find a burn?'

'Just keep going down the hill until you come out of the weather or find a path.'

'I might walk down into a valley surrounded by mountains; no path, no river, what then?'

'You ask too many questions.'

What he said, however, was sound. I have tried it when stung by my ignorance of the weather and, nearly always,

74

after descending a few hundred feet, have found myself in clearer air.

One travels light in the hills, rod, reel, line and leader all set up. A box of flies and essentials in a small bag or deep coat pocket make an untroublesome load. The coat is essential and it must be a good one, no matter how fine the weather back at the lodge or hotel. I will not discuss footwear, for, though important, it is a matter of taste and opinions vary.

The highest lochs I know that fish well lie at about 1,400 feet. At this height winters are terribly harsh and a loch might be totally frozen over for four or five months of the year. High on the Torridon sandstone and gneiss there are beds of Cambrian limestone, the most ancient of fossiliferous rocks, all over Sutherland. A loch lying on such a bed, with some depth to protect its stock of trout from hard frost, can hold fish of remarkable size despite its altitude. Higher than this and we are on the precipitous fells and crags that lurch up to the great north-western peaks. Above 1,500 feet we are in mountaineer's country, not really for the man with the rod; but it is something that all fit fly-fishers should attempt. Climbing up there at 2 or 3,000 feet on a clear day, we are soon above the shouldering hills. Heather gives way to mosses and then only lichens on the hard gneiss. We pick out the monsters of the sky-line, Foinaven, Stack Polly, brooding Hope; farther south lie Ross's giants, Eighe, Alligan and Slioch's broad spear-head. Beyond our treasured lochs and the distant hills, the sea shimmers and the Inner Hebrides lurk in brilliant waters. Farther still, away across the Minches, the outer system curves like a shield against the Atlantic. We see our lochs as the osprey sees them and the troubles of a world gone berserk seem impossibly far away.

A fly-fisher in the hills is elemental man. He has shed the niceties of civilisation. A rod is hardly an encumbrance to the man who knows trout; it is more an extension of his limbs, a thing of animal-like beauty as it bows with the weight of a good line. The nine-foot carbon fibre rod I use has replaced a little Hardy in glass fibre and before that a supple split-cane. Each one has been lighter and more delicate than the last, but they have all been suited to hill loch fishing because they have been relatively soft-actioned and matched to a light line. It is essential in our sport to approach it with tackle appropriate to the fish. Our quarry in the hills ranges from ¼ lb to 2 lbs in weight. Seldom do we catch trout heavier than this on any loch other than those on the limestone or those which are enriched by alluvial deposits. A three-pounder from the hills might be considered the equivalent of a six- or seven-pounder from the super-rich lakes of southern England or western Ireland. As Colonel H. A. Oatts put it in his classic work *Loch Trout*: 'The loch mind is the mind of a man who prefers a basket of half-pounders from the hills to a twenty-pounder from behind the gas works – and there are many such men!' Well, quite, but we fish in beautiful places in England, far from any industrial eyesore, and catch big trout; although Grafham, Rutland, the winding Test, even the tumbling waters of the Cornish streams, are all overshadowed by the Highlands.

Nearly all I have learnt in fly-fishing has been a one-way process: that is, my discoveries in Scotland have been put into practice in England. The dry fly, shortlining patterns of traditional wet fly, dapping with imitations of wind-fall insects, the single wet fly on a long line in the dark, were all revealed to me in the north. The main exception is the nymph. Very few fishers in the Highlands ever use the nymph and yet on the hill lochs it is a highly efficient method. Here in the land of tradition, I suppose, it is incongruous to fish any but the classic styles of our forefathers. There is no doubt, however, that the nymph, as popularised by Sawyer on the English chalk and then developed on stillwaters by true giants in the sport like Commander C. F. Walker and Arthur Cove, will, tomorrow, be the classic approach.

There were early pioneers of the method in Scotland. R. C. Bridgett, in his book *Loch Fishing in Theory and Practice*, describes the use of spider patterns as representations of sub-aquatic insect forms. By and large, however, the fly-fishers north of the border adopted the older styles and even now fishing the nymph is relatively scarce.

Many years ago I arrived in Kinlochewe in August after an exciting early summer on Grafham. I was wholly intoxicated with the nymph and I resolved to leave the boat at Loch Maree for a few days and walk up into the hills to try for loch trout. The first day was calm and sunny and even as I climbed the wind was slight. To the south of Kinlochewe, on the hills that merge Glen Torridon with Glen Dochertie, there is a meshwork of rugged lochs at between 1,100 and 1,300 feet. To reach them entails a steep climb from the Maree basin which is only a little above sea-level. The view is tremendous up there. Looking north we see the shining gorge of Loch Maree between Slioch and Beinn Eighe; to the west our stare scans the River Kinlochewe all the way up to Loch Clair beneath Sgurr Dubh and Beinn Alligan.

The range is called Feithe an Leothaid with its highest point at Bidein Clann Raonaild, and the old one-inch-to-the-mile Ordnance maps mark thirty-five lochs spread over two square miles. The blood in my ears was surging and my heart pounding from the effort of the climb as I reached the water. I made my way to one of the larger lochs, sat down and watched. I had chosen an upwind shore and there was a curl of calm water reaching out from the bank until the ripple started, perhaps ten yards out.

Trout were splashing, here and there, and I noticed some small brown sedges fluttering above the surface. Conditions absolutely cried out for the use of a nymph. I tied a Pheasant Tail on the point and a Sedge Pupa on a dropper, both in size 10 or 12 to match the size of the hatching flies.

One must be highly mobile when loch fishing. On southern lakes we might stay in one place for long periods because rainbows and brown trout frequently approach and pass through. On the hill lochs, except at times of maximum activity, the trout move less and tend to adopt lies, according to their size and nature. There is a distinct 'pecking order', the larger, older fish inheriting the richest or safest grounds. The static fly-fisher has his best chance during the first few casts. Thereafter, the disturbance he invariably makes as he casts and retrieves is bound to frighten all but the midget trout which, anyway, he does not want to catch.

I began fishing while I walked slowly along a 200-yard length of shore, full of the character of high lochs: points, little bays, reed beds, rocky screes. I paused where I had seen fish moving or at places which looked a good lie. Sometimes I cast only a few yards out among boulders or into holes in the weed, then I shot out twenty-five yards of line over gravelly reefs. I allowed the nymphs a moment to sink and then retrieved with slow, 'sedge-like' draws. I suspect that these trout had never seen an artificial nymph, for in two hours' fishing, as I circumnavigated the loch and one of its neighbours, I had perhaps thirty takes and beached ten fine trout at an average weight of about ½ lb.

The best fish came from the end of a line of boulders that ran into the loch. There was some deeper water just off this point. I allowed the nymphs to sink well down and then lifted them very slowly. Simultaneously I saw the line tip dart away and felt a hammer blow through the rod. The trout stayed deep for two or three minutes before I drew him in towards the boulders and the net. He was a perfect golden bar of a fish, weighing 1¼ lbs, and was heavily marked, with the Pheasant Tail firmly wedged in the scissors of his jaws. He was returned, along with seven others from the catch. There is no point in over-killing and a brace of half-pounders makes a mouthwatering and perfectly adequate breakfast for two, grilled with tomatoes and mushrooms.

On a subsequent visit to these lochs with a friend we found the trout eagerly snapping up insects, both aquatic and wind-falls, from the surface. On this occasion we tied up small Greenwell's dry flies and proceeded to face the challenge of hooking rapidly rising trout. A fraction of a second too late on the strike and the fish would spit out the fly; a moment too fast and the Greenwell's would be whipped out of its mouth.

Despite the limited amount of time one has to make a judgment, it is necessary when using dry fly for loch trout to have an idea of the size of the rising fish and the direction in which it is travelling. Large trout tend to rise more sedately than half-pounders and must be given more time to turn down. A rather fortunate factor here is that heavy trout usually rise with precise purpose. They rarely miss a fly, at least accidentally, and they take it well. Provided they are given time to turn over and down they are nearly always hooked. Young trout, with their dazzling whirl and splash of a rise, are far more difficult to judge; but they are all tremendous fun. On this particular day the two of us fished for the early part of the afternoon on three of the lochs. We lost count of the rises but it must have been approaching forty. We beached about twenty half-pounders.

It is a curious phenomenon that nymph and dry fly often attract the heavier fish from the hill lochs. Perhaps this is because these methods give presentations and movements that more closely resemble the food forms of trout. One cannot, of course, be firm on this point. Of the hundreds of lochs a fly-fisher might visit in the hills he will never find two the same; and on any water the conditions which favour the nymph one day might the next necessitate the use of traditional wet fly. Constant changes occur in the light and the wind, the temperature and pressure, all of which affect the mood of both quarry and hunter. One cannot say, with any certainty, 'This is the way to catch loch trout.' Only an impressionistic painting can be brushed from the background of a thousand images that guide the enterprising fisher in the hills.

The lie of the land surrounding a loch gives away many of the secrets which are hidden beneath the water surface. Knowing this we can build up an imagined topographical map of the loch bed. Since we cannot see the bottom, except for perhaps two or three yards out from where we are standing, we cannot be precise; but a general idea can be gleaned from the character of the shore. Precipitous cliffs rising from the surface indicate deep water close in. Points continue out into the loch, forming shallow ridges with deeper water to either side of them. Adjacent points, either across bays or from one side of the loch to another, are often connected underwater, thus forming a continuous reef. Gently sloping land by a shore implies extensive shallows, particularly where a burn or river flows into the loch from flattish country. Alluvial deposits can reach far out into the loch. High in the hills, of course, silt deposition is slight compared with the valley lochs. Islands mark huge areas of shallows surrounding them, whereas steeply contoured shores imply excessive depth. It is reasonable to expect that a ridged shore will mean that there are ridges under the water.

Given that the ideal depth for trout during most of the day is between four and twelve feet, possibly with the sanctuary of deep water near by, it is important for the fly-fisher to be able to recognise such places. Furthermore, at dawn and dusk, big trout are frequently found hunting in water no deeper than is required to cover their backs. Nearly every area where fish lie, or where they are likely to visit, may be found by careful observation. Some are obvious, others rather more subtle.

All over the Highlands are found dry-stone walls (the practice of their construction is now virtually at a standstill). They are silent signs of the time before the Clearances and a reminder of the steady depopulation of northern Scotland. These walls marked out the perimeters of crofts and served to prevent cattle and sheep straying. Besides the history they reflect, they are of significance to the fly-fisher. When they run down to the shores of lochs it is virtually certain that they carry on underwater. The walls were constructed out into the loch in order to prevent cattle wading around them. The tumbled stones of the old walls are favourite haunts of trout. Salmon, which lie in shallower water than trout, are also attracted to the walls, although this is only of concern if salmon have access to the loch (I have never found a loch higher than about 350 feet to hold migratory fish).

Woodland that approaches or overhangs the waterline is also attractive to trout. Not only does it give shade from the sun and shelter from violent storms, but it yields a supply of terrestrial insects that find their way into the loch. Deciduous copses of birch, rowan, ash, beech and oak are best in terms of the insects they attract, though only birch and the ubiquitous Scots pine reach any height into the hills. The plantations of conifers so favoured by the Forestry Commission are next to useless for insects, and indeed for wild-life in general.

Weed beds are a significant surface feature which indicate the whereabouts of trout. Weeds are larders containing insects and crustacea, as well as amphibians which are also eaten by trout, particularly in the tadpole stage.

Inflowing and outflowing burns nearly always attract fish. Feed is concentrated where water flows out of a loch or where a burn might carry insects or general carrion from the hill into the loch. In very hot weather a burn with any water in it, preferably cold from a spring in rock strata above the loch, will have a higher oxygen concentration than the tepid stillwaters and is bound to draw trout. Those burns which ooze out of soggy moorland are detrimental to the loch, for they are acid. The stream that gushes from the mountains is good, particularly if it spills through wooded gorges. Best of all are the gravelly burns that pour not too steeply into the loch. These are the ones that the trout will ascend in November to breed, though at any time of the summer and autumn they form good lies, gravel bars and spits, where their flow begins to fade in the stillwater.

Wading is usually unnecessary in the hill lochs. Indeed it can be adverse to good fishing. A man in the water cannot help but create some disturbance which will send our wild quarry flitting away into the deep. There are a few lochs I know, however, which demand that I carry a pair of waders when I fish them. One of these is a water called Loch nam Breac Buidge which is set on flat moor about half a mile west of the Borgie Forest. Though large, about three-quarters of a mile long and up to half a mile wide, it is extremely shallow, rather like many of the Caithness lochs. I doubt that it is deeper than twelve or fourteen feet at any one point, though there may be some holes out towards the middle. Despite this loch being situated on open heather moor, it is not acidic and I believe it is spring-fed from more alkaline rock. This is a desolate place and the loch is said to be haunted by some lonely spirits of people who died at the time of the Clearances. I have never met these sorry souls. The local fly-fishers claim that nam Breac Buidge is a dour water and it is rarely fished. From the moment I first saw its clean gravel and teeming insect life I knew it must hold some heavy trout. Since the loch is so shallow it demands the use of a long line from a wading fisher and I think it is for this reason that it is rarely given much attention. There is no boat.

Lying only four miles from the Atlantic and having no high hills to protect it, the water is whipped by furious winds from the north and west. In a light breeze, however, the fishing is superb. Lacking any trees within half a mile and no burns to speak of, the loch none the less has all the other features – bays, points, extensive shallows, clear calcium-rich water and weed beds – that make it ideal for trout. I often wonder, however, at the fact that the fish stocks are not savagely reduced by severe winters, as there are no deeps in which to take refuge from extreme cold. I suspect the answer lies in the springs which push water of a constant temperature into the loch throughout the year.

Wading is not too difficult, whereas on many hill lochs it is positively dangerous. In places one can wade out as far as fifty yards from the bank. Also there are big boulders strewn among the bays. The bed is made up mostly of smaller boulders and gravel.

The smallest trout that I have seen from nam Breac Buidge weighed ½ lb and the average is about 1 lb. They are fish of great beauty. In Gaelic the name means loch of the yellow, or golden, trout. They are pale, subtly rather than heavily marked and shine like unsullied gold. One rarely has a huge catch here (four or five trout in several hours' concentrated fishing being common in reasonable conditions), but this is one of a very few lochs in the area where a two- or three-pounder is likely to be among the bag at the end of the day.

Five years ago I spent one of many afternoons pursuing

these fighting trout. The season was fading and the loch's
ghosts must have been sad, for a grey sky swirled and the
wind's doleful song murmured through long banks of
heather. I was alone and feeling perhaps a little introspec-
tive. As I cleared the last hills I could see the loch and it
cheered me, like meeting an old and close friend. I walked
along the widening foreshore towards a little bay I knew.
The sun was glimpsing through the clouds and warmth
seeped in patches across the moor. Just before I started to
fish an angry cry filled the air and I thought, 'Oh God, the
ghosts,' but it was only a great skua, black against the sky,
harrying a northern diver and her two grown-up chicks.

I fished for one hour, enjoying the pleasure of curling
out a long line. I had tied up a single size 12 Pheasant Tail,
dressed with a long, thin thorax and short abdomen. In
this style it is a pretty fair imitation of the dark corixae that
abound in this water. As I waded quietly along the shore I
saw few trout, and I was beginning to believe that the loch
was in one of its truly dour moods when suddenly the line
jerked savagely. Before I knew it, a trout was airborne and
flaying at the surface. He rushed past me towards the
bank, almost beaching himself on the shingle. Then he
tore through some thin rushes and back out into the loch.
In terms of speed and acrobatics he was more like a
sea-trout; but brown trout in shallow water are a law unto
themselves and seem to unleash the demon within them.
He weighed 2 lbs 5 oz, was stuffed with corixae and was
everything a wild trout should be.

According to anatomical classification there is no difference between a brown trout, sea-trout or any of the other
trout we catch in the Highlands, such as gillaroos, ferox
and estuary trout. They are all *salmo trutta*. Fly-fishers
know them by all their different names because their
appearances are so varied. Scientifically the differences are
said to be adaptive, the colours and shape of *trutta* in a

particular loch being due to the characteristics of that environment. Well, that may be so, but on Highland estates it used to be the case that a few lochs were stocked with trout from elsewhere – Loch Levens were a favourite – and persistence of the appearance of the non-native stock can still be seen today, many, many trout-generations later. There even appears to be no interbreeding, as though the various types of trout are distinct, non-mixing races. Perhaps it is that the non-natives occupy a niche in the loch similar to their ancestral waters whereas the natives exist in a different one; although it is a peculiar phenomenon.

In this chapter I have described the essential nature of the hill loch, both in general terms and with the specific examples of two distinct types; the small lochs in high country and the larger, shallow basins on the open moor, often known as plateau lochs. Between these characteristic limits of loch and lochan forms we find an entire spectrum of waters.

In my discussion I have been heavily biased towards the nymph. In the hills, of course, the traditional wet fly has a curious magic all of its own, born from a mixture of its classic style and its effectiveness in attracting wild trout. We should understand, however, that nymph and wet fly represent different poles of the same overall style. Just as the 'pure' nymph cannot be fished properly from a drifting boat, neither is the bank perfectly suited to fully exploiting the traditional style. Nowadays so few hill lochs have boats on them that I have left this subject to the next chapter which considers the valley lochs where boat fishing is more commonly undertaken.

We have privacy in the hills, and one's approach to loch trout is personal. We are mastered by our instincts, while the ridiculous posturings of the men who tell us how we *should* be approaching our quarry are as nothing on the wind-blown moors. Coming down from high country the

85

ways of civilisation reclaim us. But the loudness and abrasiveness of human society can never destroy the memory of the enormous physical and emotional energy we shed in the hills. A part of one's soul is left out there in the wild country, though we also bring something back with us; intangible, a little frightening, finally overpowering, as it draws us back to seek fresh jewels beneath the mountains.

7

Valley Lochs and the Classic Style

STRATH, IN GAELIC, means broad valley, while glen is simply a valley. Both are always associated with a river or loch system. These are the most prized of brown trout waters in northern Scotland because they tend to be large expanses and hold prolific stocks of fish. As with the hill lochs, so the huge sheets of water of the glens seem to be around every other turn of the road or path. These lochs have easier access than those in high country and on most of them are angling club or, more commonly, hotel boats. Non-residents can hire the boats, although residents have priority. Only during the six weeks spanning the middle of July to the end of August is there sometimes difficulty in obtaining a few days on the most famous of these lochs; but even then there are always slightly less prestigious waters available that still offer fine sport. We should be thankful, in fact, that most estates have limited the number of boats on even the larger lochs. On Loyal, for example, which is four miles in length, there are between six and eight boats. I have never seen more than two or three out at any one time on this lovely mountain-flanked water. I am quite sure that an increase in fishing pressure would severely damage the fishing, though probably only in the short term. One has only to observe the high number of boats moored by the loughs of southern and western Ireland to see the good sense of the general policy in Scotland.

Here we are in country where the traditional wet fly reigns supreme. Although the sport from the shore can still be excellent, the drifting boat affords the best of the fishing on these large waters. As on the English lakes and reservoirs, the boat offers mobility and new water at every cast, together with access to islands and reefs which are impossible for the bank fisher to reach. Added to this is the fact that the classic style on lochs can only be exploited to the full from a drifting boat.

There is no typical example of this kind of loch, although they all occur in valleys or, at most, on low-lying plateaus with well-defined, usually large, basins. Neither are they restricted to the mainland. They are common in the Inner Hebrides, though in the outer isles, which are hilly rather than mountainous, the lochs more closely resemble those in the high regions of Sutherland and Ross, except that they are close to sea-level.

From county to county, even in different valleys, the waters change in their character. Loyal, with steeply rising mountains on all sides, is quite unlike the huge Rimsdale chain on the moor above the River Helmsdale. Loch Brora on the lush, but less dramatic, east coast of Sutherland is incomparable with the rugged nature of Loch Assynt in the west, or Loch Meadie in Strath More. That all these lochs yield to the fly some of the finest wild brown trout fishing in the world is, of course, their common thread.

The valley waters are often sea-trout and salmon lochs which are the subject of the next chapter. Those which contain brown trout and no migratory fish are usually far from the sea or they are isolated by rivers which are either too steep or blocked by large waterfalls which the migrants cannot navigate. The falls on the River Borgie, for example, are rarely ascended by sea-trout, though salmon habitually do so. Consequently the lochs at the head of the River Borgie – Slaim, Craggie and Loyal – all have a run of salmon into them. Loch Naver, though some distance from the sea, has a good run of both salmon and sea-trout owing to there being no impassable falls on the slowly running River Naver.

The closer a freshwater loch lies to the sea, and the shorter the connecting river, the less likely it is to be purely a brown trout water. Many, however, are noted more for their resident stock than for migrants.

The range of possibilities for the fly-fisher, adrift on the lochs, is vast. On any but the smallest of these waters only a fraction of the holding areas can be sampled in a single day. On Loch Loyal I estimate that a fisher would need a fortnight, at least, even to begin to know the range of drifts in the southernmost two miles, and only then if weather conditions were favourable. Other large waters, such as the Rimsdale chain, where the best drifts may be less easily defined, would take far longer to get to know. But this is all part of the humbling process that leaves a fly-fisher wondering at just how little of the water space in northern Scotland he has sampled. One lifetime is a hundred-fold too short and the years speed past, leaving us frustrated in our ignorance, certain only that we have had to leave so much to the unknown.

The reading of the water is essentially the same as in the hills, albeit on an enlarged scale. Given that we fish from a boat, the range of water which now interests the fly-fisher is far greater than on the high lochs. Distant island shallows can be approached, as can reefs and other submarine features like dead trees washed down by winter floods; also weed beds that may or may not break the surface a hundred yards or more from the nearest shore. We can venture to those places where a bank fisher dares not go, such as rocky screes, beneath which there may be ledges or built-up landslides at the right depth for trout; or shores unapproachable by foot because of bogs or rivers, or simply because of their distance from the nearest road.

An irritating feature known to all shore fishers is the extensive area of shallow water, on a bank or in a bay, which means that most of the trout will be beyond casting range for much of the time. I know of dozens of lochs where the best fishing is quite inaccessible from the shore. Even careful wading creates a disturbance which is much greater than the near perfection of a quietly drifted boat. It is a curious and fortunate fact that a boat guided by the wind, with occasional, unhurried strokes of the oars for correcting the line of drift, does not frighten trout or salmon. Fish can be risen within feet of the boat and, once hooked, seek refuge beneath the hull. What is equally true, however, is that a man who stands up, particularly when there is a clear or bright sky, ceases to be a part of the boat and will continue to frighten trout of any size and sense for as long as he remains upright.

It may seem obvious to say that a tidy, dry boat is a dream to fish from, whereas one in which water sloshes around in the bottom, with nails and bits of wood poorly fastened, is a nightmare. It is a feature of our times, with labour being so costly, that boats on many Highland lochs are kept in a poor state of repair. This is even the case on some of our most famous sea-trout lochs – Maree at Kinlochewe is an exception in that the boats here are kept to the highest standards – but on the brown trout lochs, where rents for the fishing are low, hoteliers and fishery managements find little money for the upkeep of their boats. On many lochs nowadays the boats are left out all winter, albeit upturned on the shore, to suffer the destruction of severe weather. There have been many occasions when I have arrived with friends at a loch to find our boat half-awash with seepage water. It can take half an hour to bail out a boat and remove from it numerous hazards, such as broken and rotten floor-boarding and the oft-curious flotsam that is collected. It is worth taking with you a spare set of universal rowlocks, for if these are not supplied by the hotel it is surprising just how frequently they are missing from a boat, having been 'borrowed' by uncharitable fishers. A boat without rowlocks is useless. A pair can be rigged up with a good baler twine as an emergency substitute. Furthermore, poorly kept vessels will invariably have to be bailed fairly frequently during the course of a day's fishing.

It is a common practice nowadays to replace ruined wooden boats with low-maintenance constructions in glass-fibre. This too is sad because, though highly manoeuvrable, they drift far too fast for correct fly presentation in anything of a wind, and in a storm they are positively dangerous. Having said this, I suppose that messing around in boats is all part of the boyish fun to be had from fly-fishing; although as age creeps along the quality of the sport can be marred somewhat by an unreliable boat.

The ideal boat is constructed in wood and is fairly heavy. At Maree, Peter Macdonald, who lives in the village of Kinlochewe, has two boats on the loch. They are of good design and both are in excellent condition and I have used them throughout the past fifteen years. One of them, *Salar*, is as close to perfection as can be achieved in a fishing boat; slow drifting with virtually no stern bias, large and uncluttered. Furthermore, Peter's boats are kept to such a high standard that in dry weather, or if no water slops over the gunwales in more stormy conditions, they need not be bailed for days on end. How my fishing companions and I lament the loss of such fine vessels from so many of the Scottish waters!

Once afloat the task of finding trout begins. It is quite possible, and I have seen it done time after time, for a thoughtlessly placed boat to drift for most of the day over water in which there is little hope of finding fish. On a hugh loch the omnipresent spectre of continuous acreages threatens the fly-fisher. The inexperienced man in a boat can cast aside good sense and play a sort of roulette: 'This looks a pretty drift, we'll try here.' And so a fruitless day passes inconsequentially by. The 'loch mind', as Colonel Oatts calls it, must be engaged and fed. I have heard, perhaps a thousand times, that fishing the lochs is largely a matter of chance. If conditions are good then we might be lucky if we happen upon the right fly. But those who say this about fishing for loch trout have missed the whole point of the sport and do not understand it. To perform well and successfully on a loch requires more mental exertion than any branch of fly-fishing I know, except possibly the use of the nymph from the bank and pursuit of big sea-trout on very large lochs.

As instinct is developed and knowledge is gathered, the element of chance dwindles in fly-fishing. It never completely disappears because the difference between a big trout boated and one that sheds the hook just before the net is down to luck; similarly the red-letter day will be just a throw of the dice away from one of an average catch. By and large, however, over a season at least, chance does not play a major role.

We seek out our quarry on the valley waters just as we do in the hills; by studying the lie of surrounding terrain, finding weed beds and burns and interesting features of the loch. Local knowledge helps and good ghillies can quickly take you to rich areas. In recent years I prefer not to fish with ghillies, with the exception of a few who have become friends, or those rare older ones with wonderful stories to tell. Some wise person once said: 'It is better to lose on your own terms than win on somebody else's.' In a fishing boat controlled by a ghillie it is less the fly-fisher's skill that catches the fish and more the ghillie's own knowledge and control of the drift. Besides, there are very few first-rate ghillies left nowadays. Like the good, wooden drift-boats, they are a breed which is rapidly dying out.

In general terms we aim for water between four and fourteen feet in depth for as long a drift as possible. Obviously wind direction determines the length of all drifts. The wind blowing along a shoreline might enable us to drift for a considerable distance, whereas an onshore wind necessitates a zig-zagging series of short drifts if the same area is to be properly covered. In mountain-flanked valleys where the waters are of the rift valley or, more commonly, the glacier-formed type, the wind is often channelled by the high country to blow conveniently along the shore. Loyal is a perfect example of this sort of loch. Although it lies north to south, winds from other quarters are frequently curled around the mountains to blow along Loyal's rich shores. On more open waters, or those which are more heavily featured by points and islands, the drifts must be picked out with respect to wind direction. Premier trout water can render a poor return to one's efforts if the wind is wrong, requiring the boat to be over-frequently corrected in its drift or in a clumsy line of approach. Conversely, water of little note can produce unexpected catches if unusual winds allow a good drift.

No shore will have a perfect wind all of the time. In

order to maintain a boat above the ideal depth it is necessary, now and then, to give a 'touch of the oar'. This is the main function nowadays of a ghillie, but with practice it is easy enough to do it yourself while still fishing with the other hand. A strong, but quiet, pull or push on an oar can make the difference between maintaining the boat, with rods, on fishable water and having it floating over barren depths. If the force of the wind increases, it is more difficult simultaneously to hold the boat and fish a good line. The ghillie really comes into his own here, manoeuvring the vessel slowly down a drift while waves stamp against the hull.

If one is alone in a boat, a drogue become necessary in a wind greater than a force 4. Only then can the flies be fished slowly enough for consistent effect. It is a waste of time to thunder along across the loch while our offerings flash about in the waves. Even if a trout sees the flies they will be whipped away before he has a chance of rising to them. The main problem with using a drogue is that navigation of the boat becomes impossible; one can do no more than drift straight downwind with perhaps the slightest swing if the drogue is on a long rope and the boat has a bow or stern bias. When alone, therefore, in strong winds, it is best to find extensively shallow areas where trout may be expected to be dispersed and over which the drogue-held boat can drift for a reasonable length of time. With two fishers in the same boat, the problem of strong winds is minimised if turns are taken at the oars while only one rod fishes.

The time-honoured way of drifting broadside to the wind – that is with the keel of the boat perpendicular to the wind's direction – is part of the classic style. There is a growing tendency for fishers to hang a drogue either from the stern or from the bows, which moves the keel along the line of the breeze. The rods then cast across the wind, one each side of the boat. This method has grown from lure fishing tactics on the reservoirs in the Midlands and is called the 'Northampton style'. It is now practised widely in England where it is deadly for rainbow trout. An inductive movement is imparted to the flies as the boat's motion drags the line into a curve behind and away from the boat. There is no doubt that this method is successful but I would suggest that it has no place on a Highland loch. It is only one step away from trolling, and has many inherent faults which make it usually less successful than the broadside drift when fishing for wild trout, particularly sea-trout. What it does do is to make it easier for those who, demanding little from their sport, are content to take run-of-the-mill fish.

So much has been written about the traditional wet fly that it seems impertinent of me to add anything more. I will merely consider the method in the context of northern trout lochs and make some points drawn from my observations over the seasons. For me it is the most beautiful style in fly-fishing, both to watch and to perform. I have seen some highly talented exponents of the genre at work, mostly in Scotland, though occasionally in England, and I have spent many an hour in Highland hotel bars talking to these wizards of the loch. One comes to realise that they are the only true experts in our strange craft, the silent men with few boasts, who seek no financial profit from their skill, only the sort of gain a fisher accepts rather than takes as he becomes in tune with big waters.

I once had the following conversation with an elderly married couple, both highly skilled with the wet fly. They came every year to fish a large loch in the area.

'Are you going out tomorrow?' I asked.

'Yes, we hope so,' replied the woman, 'it will be good tomorrow.'

'Well, if conditions stay like this it might.'

'They will,' interjected her husband. 'I can feel it in the air. Do you know,' he continued with a sparkle in his humorous old eyes, 'we saw two good big fellows today, one off Broc Point and the other by the old tree. Didn't chuck at them, light was all wrong; but we'll try for them tomorrow.' The loch we were talking about was noted for a good stock of trout of about 1 lb. Only rarely was a fish heavier than 2 lbs caught there.

'How big do you think they were?'

The lady replied without pause for thought. 'The one off the Point was 3 lbs, the other nearer 4.'

'Goodness, I should have been tempted to cast at them today.' But somehow I suspected that they knew better.

The following day I went off to a sea-trout loch and hardly gave the couple a thought. On returning to the hotel I met their ghillie and asked how they had fared.

'Only the two,' he said.

'Oh, any size?'

'3 lbs 2 ozs and 4 lbs exactly!'

As if this was not enough, he went on to tell me that they had only gone out for an hour in the morning; the woman, who caught the heavier fish, had cast a total of three times, while her husband had delivered his flies during the brief period of the boat drifting in towards the Point. They had then picnicked by the loch and ambled off together for a gentle walk in the hills. That, I thought, was good fishing.

The word 'team' is widely used to describe the collection of flies on a wet cast. Most fishers apply the word purely as a collective term; but it is more than this. Team implies a group working together for a shared purpose and this is more exactly the meaning of a team of flies. The purpose, of course, is obvious, but it is the 'working together' that is so fascinating. The team must be balanced, both in terms of the chosen patterns and in the weights and dimensions of the flies. The balancing of a team is a subject in itself and is perhaps best understood by firstly considering the types of fly, then their dynamic properties – the way in which they move or can be made to move – and finally their combination in a team.

There must have been many thousands of traditional wet flies invented during the long history of fly-fishing; but the really famous ones, often named so evocatively, number perhaps a hundred. These are the tried and tested flies that have persisted through generations of fly-fishers to become traditional patterns. Every trout man has his favourites and often some of his own design, dressed in the accepted style, in which he has total trust. They fall into two broad categories: general imitative patterns and 'attractors'. The latter tend to be brighter and more flashy, often resembling fish fry, and will induce the killing instinct in a trout. The more imitative flies are loose representations, usually in duller and more natural colours, of a trout's food forms.

Certain patterns are peculiarly attractive to trout in given conditions and others are consistent over a wider range of circumstances. There are fishers who believe the choice of fly is relatively unimportant and that presentation is the key. My own experience tells me that both the fly and its mode of action in the water are vital, and that some flies, to work best, require quite a different presentation from others.

Fished fast, all flies become attractors in that they lose any resemblance to natural insects – except possibly hatching sedge or the whirling rise and fall of corixae – while the brighter patterns, when drawn slowly through the water, might well be taken by a trout in mistake for one of its natural items of food. Of course even the imitative patterns are not the close copies of insects that we attempt to produce with artificial nymphs, but they certainly contain qualities that we believe deceive a trout rather than incite in it purely an aggressive reaction. The long, dark legs and segmented body, perhaps also the wisp of a tail, of a Pennell cutting through the surface film gives, to the fisher's eyes at least, an enticing impression of a hatching fly.

There are few flies that fit conveniently into either of the categories. Those which are obviously attractors might include the Dunkeld, Butcher, Zulu and Peter Ross, while the Mallard and Grouse series, the March Brown, Hare's Ear and Sooty Olive, are much closer to the insect-imitative style. But there are any number of flies that are intermediate in nature; the Green Peter, Soldier Palmer and the Teal series, to name but a few.

There are those fishers who claim that attractor style wet flies are simply mini-lures, or rather that the lure fishing methods were derived from the fast wet fly. So be it; although there seems to me to be a world of difference between a Dunkeld dressed on a size 12 or 10 hook fished in the classic style, and a black lure dressed on something the size of a salmon iron stripped back on a fast-sinking line. It is a matter of scale, I suppose, and one or two other things besides.

Colour, or perhaps shade, of a wet fly plays a significant role in its ability to catch trout. Shape is probably just as important, at least to the extent that this is one of the qualities which will determine how a fly sinks and subsequently moves in the water. Bulky dressings on un-weighted hooks have poor penetration through the surface film unless there is a good wave. Thereafter their rate of sinking is very slow. Sparse dressings, especially those incorporating soft materials like hen hackles and wool, cut through the surface and sink rapidly. Stiff hackles, splayed out from the dressing, also retard a fly's rate of fall through the water, as will any material that is buoyant or that traps air in its fibres. Hook size and the density of the wire from which hooks are constructed are the most important factors in determining how fast or slowly a fly will sink.

Some patterns are traditionally fished for best results in certain places on the team. Pennells, for example, are ideally suited to the dropper positions. Conversely, flies like the Peter Ross tend to be tail flies. To dress a Pennell on a heavy hook, or a Peter Ross with a bulky dressing on a light hook would throw a team containing both completely out of balance. Diagrams 4 and 5 show one of the differences between balanced and imbalanced teams.

In Diagram 4 a sparse tail fly, dressed on a heavier hook than either of the droppers, has dragged the cast down to the ideal position from which to begin a retrieve. Even the top dropper is dressed reasonably sparsely in order to prevent it from floating and causing 'skating' during the

A balanced team
– a heavy and sparsely dressed tail fly
on a substantial wire hook

Diagram 4

99

A poorly balanced team
– the tail fly is both too light and too bulky;
the top dropper is too heavy

Diagram 5

retrieve. In Diagram 5 everything is wrong. The tail fly is both too light and too bulky and it retards the fluid fall of the team. Also it is floating and will skate as the line is tightened. Far from attracting trout, this team will frighten them unless there is a good wave to hide the imperfections.

One occasionally hears a tail fly being referred to as a stretcher, which is a very good description and leads to the next point of balancing a three-fly cast. Given that heavy wire hooks drag the team beneath the surface, they then, as the retrieve begins, act as sea-anchors or drogues. The tail fly should be on the heaviest hook, stretching out the team, itself remaining deeper than the other flies. The angle of approach of the flies to the surface is important, particularly in the case of the top dropper. A tail fly of the correct weight forces the droppers to approach at the required angle as the fisher raises the rod.

There is, if you think about it, a beautiful geometry associated with fly-fishing. In no method is this more true than in shortlining. Diagram 6 demonstrates this particular geometry. I call it the Shortlining Triangle. The triangle is not perfect because the sagging line, the flex of the rod and the wave on the water are not straight lines. None the less, ideally the team moves during the retrieve much in the way shown.

The last major factor when balancing a team concerns the mixing of fly patterns. This is probably the most intangible of the points and, in the end, it must come down to personal choice. The logic of the matter stems from a mixture of judging a trout's aggressive nature and the position of a fly in the water which will be most likely to entice a fish. Here we must adopt the trout's mind. We see a fly close to the surface, apparently escaping. That might be enough to launch us into the attack, for we might simply be hungry. But then we notice the tail fly of a

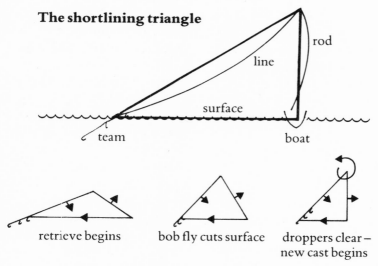

The shortlining triangle

rod

line

surface

team   boat

retrieve begins   bob fly cuts surface   droppers clear –
                                              new cast begins

Arrows show direction of relative movement

Diagram 6

101

team. This might appear to be another fish in pursuit of the hatching fly. In a blur of instinctive reaction we spin up to the surface, either to attack the little fish that has invaded our territory or to take the fly which otherwise our competitor will eat. Now this concept might be facile and could well be wrong; but trout are aggressive and, at times of sparse fly activity, highly competitive. I am convinced that a team of flies owes at least some of its success to the above principles. For these reasons some fishers choose imitative patterns for top droppers and attractors for the tail, with perhaps transitional patterns in the middle dropper position. Even if the theory is wrong, the system works very well in practice.

Most of us refer to a successful fly on a particular day; but I feel we should describe the whole team. It is like the footballer who scores the goal. What chance would he have had without the rest of his team? The choice of pattern and its size is dependent on the conditions, always remembering the question of balance. The following points have guided me through the years.

Bright light dazzles and confuses trout. They tend to stay deep, away from the glare, and are less willing to rise to the surface. If they are tempted to move at a fly high in the water they will be suddenly dazzled and may well miss their target. When the light is intense and the water calm I tend to use dark, fairly small flies. Dark, sombre colours show up well in bright conditions, and the fly is small because when the water is calm a large fly will create too much of a disturbance. In rough water I keep to the dark flies but use larger sizes. What is certain is that trout have good vision in low-light intensities, particularly at short range. In dull, calm weather, therefore, I use the smallest flies and dress them sparsely. Large fish are not easily deceived; if they see too much and it looks unnatural they are very unlikely to take. As the wind picks up in dull

10 Left: *Salar*, Boat Bay,
Loch Maree, 1980

11 Below: Cock sea-trout
(7 lbs), Loch Maree,
autumn 1980

12　Above: Loch Hope and Ben Hope from the north, summer 1977

13　Below: Herbert Macdonald, head ghillie, Loch Hope, summer 1981

14 Above: Salmon (11 lbs) and sea-trout (6 lbs), Loch Hope,
summer 1977
15 Below: Salmon (11 lbs) on the dap, Loch Hope, summer 1977

16 Above: Graeme Longmuir and ghillie, Loch Horisary, North Uist, autumn 1981
17 Below left: Salmon at the Borgie Falls, summer 1978
18 Below right: Sea-trout (5 lbs) about to be returned, autumn 1979

weather the size of fly can be increased. The largest flies I use, size 8s, are for wild conditions. These are also dressed with more bulk. In the spinning, tilting world of the loch's upper layers during stormy weather, a trout must often fail to see a fly. The larger patterns can sink to slightly calmer layers and will still be seen among the chaos.

Over deeper reefs, those of between twelve and fourteen feet, where one suspects there are good trout, it is wise to have one of these larger flies on the team – in the tail position. This fly will be seen by the fish and may draw them up to the surface. There they may be made wary by the fly's large size, but there is a chance that they will take one of the smaller flies on the cast. Another way of tackling the deeper fishing water requires two fishers in the boat, one of them dapping a large fly which draws the fish up, while the other fishes a team of flies, which the trout are sure to take!

One often hears that trout are 'taking short', which means they are missing the fly or merely giving it a half-hearted tweak. There are two reasons for this behaviour, and both stem from faults in the fisher rather than the mood of the trout. The first is using a fly which is too large – this is as true for dapping as for wet fly-fishing – and the second is retrieving the line too fast. I used to suffer a great deal from the phenomenon of short rising, particularly with sea-trout. Nowadays it rarely happens because I use comparatively small flies and, unless there is a very good reason for doing otherwise, a slow retrieve.

There are two ways of presenting a team of flies: classic shortlining and longlining, the latter of which is tending towards nymph fishing as performed on stillwaters. Shortlining is the most thrilling way I know of catching trout; a ten-foot rod in continuous motion, roll-casting or a single up-and-down cast, the fly line barely touching the water, then lifting while the flies hypnotise and tantalise, for all the world like hatching insects. The bob fly cuts the waves, sinks and reappears, and from the darkness a golden trout whirls, curling its flashing body as it dashes over and down. All goes tight, line and rod, and you feel the fish's strength.

Since the development of the beautifully light material of carbon fibre, there is a tendency for shortlining fishers to use longer rods than used to be the case with glass fibre or built cane. Twelve feet is becoming common in a boat fly rod. The principle of a longer rod is to allow the bob fly to be worked at the surface farther from the boat and for longer than is possible with a short rod. This much is true, although I find that a ten-foot rod, which is more comfortable in use, is perfect for the job, drawing the flies through the waves at the perfect angle and at just the right distance from the boat. Since it is also often necessary to change to casting a long line, for which a ten-footer is ideal, as conditions and the mood of the fish alter, this rod is a good compromise.

Longlining is less dependent on the boat's speed through the water. On the whole I find shortlining is best in moderate winds, while in calm weather, when a ripple rather than a good wave breaks the surface, or in uncomfortably wild weather, longlining becomes more effective. For the slow retrieve and minimal disturbance which is necessary for taking trout in quiet conditions, it becomes vital to throw a long line. In winds stronger than a force 3 or 4, the boat's rate of drift is too rapid to present the flies for a satisfactory length of time with each cast on a short line.

I remember a series of visits to Loch Craggie which lies partially divided from Loch Loyal by a narrow ridge of land. This water, a mile long and up to half a mile wide, is the epitome of a good loch for traditional wet fly styles. It has a stock of trout averaging slightly under 1 lb, with some heavy specimens among them. There are also salmon present from the very beginning of the trout season, for the River Borgie, which is fed by Loyal and Craggie, is one of the earliest salmon rivers in the north-west of Scotland.

The first day opened wild, with leaden sky and white horses speckling the water. A north-westerly rode down the loch. The boats at Craggie are moored at the southern end and, on this day, the only chance of some good shortlining was going to be under the shelter of the north shore. Therefore I made my slow way up the loch. Conditions, as it turned out, were pleasant up there and as I arrived there were breaks in the cloud. A good 'trout swell' rolled into one of the bays in the north-eastern quarter of the loch. There is a depth of twelve feet about eighty or ninety yards offshore in this bay which shelves up into the shallows by the bank. Also a large Point to the south marks the beginning of a long reef. With a northerly or north-westerly one can have seven or eight drifts into the bay and across the Point, covering new water all the time. At every cast there is the chance of rising a trout. In fact I managed eight drifts and caught nine trout averaging ¾ lb. Every rise was to one of the droppers. The weather then became furious and, with the help of the wind, I was back at the moorings in a matter of minutes. (The upwind journey had taken almost an hour.) On the following day the weather was atrocious, with constant rain and a force 5 with stronger gusts. I sought some shelter where I could and, longlining the same team as on the previous visit, managed to boat five good trout, this time all on the tail fly.

A few weeks later I returned with a friend and his son. On this occasion conditions were perfect until a little time before we packed up. The wind was again from the north-west, throwing a peaceful wave across the loch. In the bay I have described we fished for two hours. My friend and his son took turns every drift with a dapping rod while I shortlined the same faithful team as on the other days. The trout were absolutely suicidal, rising both to my companions' dapped crane-flies and my own top dropper. In that bay I counted twenty takes to my own fly and boated fourteen trout. In other places around the loch I took four or five more. The smallest was ¾ lb and the heaviest 1½ lbs. Every fish I took came to the top dropper, a Black Pennell, and I was not aware of a single rise to the other flies. As an experiment, half-way through the day, I replaced the fly I was using on the middle dropper with another Black Pennell. I rose no fish to it, while continuing to draw fish to the bob fly.

There are some lessons to be learnt from this series of visits to Craggie. I believe they were successes for two main reasons. One was that the boat spent most of the time on water where there was plenty of trout and the other was that the team was so perfectly balanced. The mood of the trout varied, resulting in their taking different flies in different positions over the three days; but the balanced cast absorbed these vagaries of a fish's mind.

There was also a spectacular incident on the last of these visits. My companions wanted a drift with the wet fly while I dapped. Half-heartedly, because I was so fascinated with the shortlining, I took the dapping rod in my right hand while I worked an oar with my left. I had just remarked that we were covering good salmon water when a fish lunged high out of the water at the crane-fly. It was certainly a salmon and, for this particular water, it was huge, weighing around 20 lbs. It went for the fly like a mako shark after mackerel. One of the main problems with dapping is that it is so reliant on the wind. On this occasion, as the salmon tore at its target, a gust of wind carried the fly a few inches too high into the air and the fish missed. It did not come back for a second attack; but I was certainly finished: I did not catch anything else that day!

8

The Sea-Trout Lochs

As WIMBLEDON IS to tennis and Lords to cricket, so Loch
Maree is to sea-trout fishing. For anyone who has had
anything to do with this sport the word Maree conjures up
evocative images of huge sea-trout on a big water. The
mighty Alaskan salmon rivers or the tumbling sea-bound
waters of west Norway might, perhaps, be comparable in
terms of beauty and sport; but nowhere could possibly
surpass Maree, and for the fly-fisher seeking large quarry
on fine tackle, almost unbearable excitement and breathtaking scenery, this west-coast loch is the pinnacle.

Historically, many of the world's heaviest sea-trout
have been caught from Loch Maree. On a wall in the sun
lounge of the hotel at Talladale is a 19-lb fish and I have
heard numerous reports of other colossal trout from the
water, one at 21 lbs and another at 22½ lbs. Of course
these were caught some time ago and details of their
capture have faded through the generations. But, for a fish

that may be considered good at 3 lbs, superb at 5 lbs and very large at 7 lbs, the double-figure fish that have been taken from Maree until recent years are outstanding. In Britain we are lucky to have inherited numerous waters than can produce sea-trout fairly commonly between 5 and 10 lbs, and a few up to 15 lbs, but I believe I am right in stating that no other fishery has produced as many of this species of such quality as Maree.

I have never caught a sea-trout of 10 lbs or more. It is one of the last ambitions in my life to do so and apparently the most fugitive. My heaviest to date is 8½ lbs and I have been lucky enough to take many approaching that weight; but the ten-pounder remains elusive. Peter Macdonald of Kinlochewe has caught two weighing over 9 lbs, one from Maree and the other from Loch Coulin which is on the Maree system. Charles C. McLaren of Altnaharra has taken several ten-pounders from Maree and at least one from Loch Hope. The two biggest sea-trout taken by men I have known were not actually caught from Maree but from Hope, which must rank a close second on the league of premier waters. These two fish were actually taken during the same week, some time back in the 1960s. The first weighed 17½ lbs and was caught on a Black Pennell (wet) fished by the late Hugh Sutherland and the second weighed 16 lbs and was caught on the dap by my old ghillie on Hope, Herbert Macdonald. The stories I have heard of these two fish make me tremble with excitement, for they were true giants. On two occasions, both on Maree, I have risen trout that my companions and I were positive were in excess of 10 lbs. These two fish came to the wet fly. Youth and an over-eager hand lost me one and the other incident I have described at the beginning of this book. Another big sea-trout that briefly came my way could well have been in excess of 10 lbs, although we never saw him clearly enough to be sure. Only his head broke the surface while his jaws engulfed a dapped crane-fly. I hooked him and he went straight to the bottom. He was extremely powerful. After five minutes the fly inexplicably came free of its hold. Ah, the ones that get away!

I have fished for sea-trout all over the British Isles, mostly in northern Scotland and the Hebrides. There are two waters I consider to be the best in the land, for reasons which are difficult to pinpoint. It has something to do with the collective qualities of large waters, which I adore: outstanding scenery, heavy migratory fish, highly variable weather and the awesome atmosphere of the north-west coast. And maybe a good deal more besides. Of course, every wide expanse of water has a character all of its own and, over the seasons, as a fly-fisher develops some little understanding of its ways, the loch becomes very special to him. For seventeen years now, I have ventured over Maree and Hope and have uncovered at least a few of their secrets. I never tire, for I know that even if I am lucky enough to have another seventeen years, or twice that, there will be much left hidden.

My enthusiasm for these lochs needs to be qualified. Neither water is always easy to fish. Far from it, for the days of light catches are numerous. On only a few days each season are the conditions perfect for the giants to move. They will take a fly at other times once one has learnt their lies and the conditions in which they might profitably be covered. I know of one veteran Maree fisher who spends much more time watching the water from the boat or the bank than he does actually fishing. Both lochs provide fairly consistent sport in terms of their average fish, between 1 and 3 lbs. The salmon in Hope come rather more readily to the fly, wet or dapped, whereas Maree's sea-trout are heavier and slightly more numerous.

Good sport with sea-trout has nothing to do with easy fishing. I know of many lochs and rivers throughout

Britain where it is far easier to make a heavy catch of sea-trout than on Maree or Hope. I have enjoyed the fishing of many loch and river systems on the mainland, as well as the smaller but sometimes ridiculously prolific waters of the Inner and Outer Hebrides; although in all my wanderings there have never been other lochs that provide quite the mixture of good sport and challenge that we find on Loch Maree and Loch Hope.

I once had a long argument with a ghillie who knew Loch Eilt fairly well but had only fished Maree for a single season.

'Eilt is a much better loch,' he claimed.

'Why do you say that?'

'More fish.'

'But Maree is bigger, full of holding water and teeming with sea-trout, most of them far heavier than the average taken from Eilt.'

He was unshakeable. 'Maree is dour; it is much easier to catch good fish on Loch Eilt.' He simply did not understand the Ross water and had missed the whole point of the sport with sea-trout. Or maybe I stubbornly hold on to dated ideals; fishers' attitudes towards this magnificent fish are highly varied and very personal.

My intention is not to over-clutter these pages with technical details concerning the capture of sea-trout. The techniques developed for enticing brown trout on large lochs are consistent with the pursuit of sea-trout in the same environment, with minor variations and extensions. The first important difference is the niche occupied by migrant trout in a freshwater loch. Those brown trout that offer sport to the true fly-fisher are seldom, if ever, found at depths exceeding twelve, or possibly fourteen, feet. The best holding water for these fish is invariably between four and twelve feet. It is often said that sea-trout lie at much greater depths than their non-migrant cousins. I will hazard that this is not completely true. Dappers often claim to take fish from drifts between twenty and thirty feet deep. Although this might be the average depth of the water they are covering, there are shallower areas — boulders and reefs — on which the sea-trout are lying. I have a strong suspicion that these fish rarely lie on the bottom thirty feet down. If they did they would be very unlikely to see any fly on the surface in the peaty waters of the north-western lochs. I would suggest that twenty feet is a more realistic maximum depth.

Sea-trout can also occupy lies that are extremely shallow, much as salmon do. This is particularly true in the early morning or late evening, though both fresh fish and staler residents will frequently patrol the shallows at other times of day, or night, even in bright weather. Essentially, then, the sea-trout fisher is exploring depths of between a few inches and twenty feet. A large dapping fly just might be able to bring fish up from deeper water.

The other difference is that migratory fish rarely feed once they have returned to freshwater. They carry what energy they require for their months away from the sea 'on their backs'. When presenting flies to sea-trout, and salmon, we do not match the creatures in the hatch, if any, because the fish are hardly ever interested. We simply incite in the trout, by carefully chosen teams and tantalising motions, the memory of the feeding response and the killing instinct. Quite why sea-trout will take a fly of the imitative type, fished very slowly, much as feeding trout will take a nymph, is uncertain, but take it they will.

I never take quite so much painstaking care with fishing tackle as I do on my arrival at Kinlochewe or the crofter's cottage I often stay at near Loch Hope. After the twelve-hour journey through the night to Wester Ross I am exhausted when finally we drive down the long glen and into Kinlochewe. After unloading, though not unpacking, I find myself back in the car and driving the two miles to the loch for a first look. That moment is very special for me. Back at Kinlochewe, after attending to family needs, the rods, lines and flies are ritually set up. With the ten-foot rod I spend ages until I am convinced that the knots are safe, the leader is of perfect length and the droppers are the correct distance apart. On go some proven patterns to make up a team as balanced as I am able to produce. This tackle is then lovingly placed on wall fastenings where it remains until the first trip out.

The equipment already set up will be the faithful standby for each day I spend on the loch. In conditions which suit shortlining it will be used continuously, with occasional changes of fly pattern and size together with slight adjustments of leader length. I then assemble the nine-foot rod which will be used in calm weather for longlining teams of two or three wet flies or a single dry fly. Finally, I set up my wife's rod which is a fifteen-foot dap. All the time that this traditional performance is being indulged, my wife is taking evasive action around the sprawl of fishing tackle, extracting our little daughter Hannah from the fly box and wondering why on earth she married a man who suffers from such regular bouts of insanity.

Regular sessions at the fly-vice follow, though in truth there are always enough flies prepared to last a year. Fishing in the Highlands on Sundays is frowned upon, although we usually sneak off to a hill loch far from the eyes of pious folk; but all the time we dream of Monday and do our share of praying – for a good fishing wind!

At dawn, on the first fishing day of the week, the boat is launched. The final restraints and responsibilities of one's other life are shed; the noise of the outboard engine dies to leave the peace of a ruffling wind chopping at the water.

And how strange is that feeling as the flies are detached from the rod, the line lengthened and the first casts in a series of thousands are made. I say to myself: 'Sea-trout at last; now where are you?'

The killer diseases of the salmonidae, namely furunculosis and UDN, swept through fisheries in the north Atlantic in the late 1960s and early 1970s and savagely depleted the fish stocks. Loch Maree did not escape the epidemics, though Hope, I believe, was relatively unscathed. From the mid 1970s onwards the diseases disappeared while sea-trout and salmon stocks gradually increased, though even in 1985 those stocks, particularly of larger fish, have not achieved the same quality as before the diseases struck. Every season on the breeding redds around Maree the trout are seen to be a little larger than the previous year, with more age groups being represented, and in larger quantities. So many of the heavy fish, however, are taken by nets and commercial poaching that it may be that we will never see a total recovery, and could again witness a decline.

In pre-disease years a five-pounder, though a fine fish, was not outstanding, while ten-pounders were caught every year. Now, it is an event when, five-, six- and seven-pounders are taken, and it has been some time since I have heard of a ten-pounder on the fly. They are there, as are bigger fish, but they are relatively scarce.

On the Kinlochewe water, which reaches a total of six miles along two shores, there are eleven places where I have taken sea-trout of over 5 lbs, together with a number from the head of the loch which is shallow over a very large area. All these places are lies, or holding points, in the loch which seem to attract the big migrants. Only two, possibly three, of these lies are noted for holding salmon. The heavier trout are occasionally encountered as they 'pass through', but this is far less common than rising them on the holding points. The head of the loch itself is probably the best water on all Loch Maree, particularly late in the season, during September and October, when it becomes concentrated with large sea-trout as they prepare to run the River Kinlochewe to the high lochs. This density of fish is probably the reason for so many of them showing – leaping, rolling and wallowing – as they challenge one another for the best lies.

In hot years with low rainfall during the summer months (1983 and 1984 were examples), the water level drops markedly. In these conditions the heavier trout adopt their lies and move around very little during the day. In wetter years, migrations to and from the holding points are frequent, particularly as fresh fish filter into the loch.

Besides the head waters, four of the lies I have mentioned are large, two are fairly small and the rest extremely small, easily missed by a drifting boat. There are certainly other holding areas, but I have yet to find them. They are probably the roofs and ridges of boulders ten feet below the surface or a ledge off the mouth of one of the numerous inflowing burns. There are also places in plenty where sea-trout of between 1 and 3 lbs are encountered.

Newcomers to Loch Maree, on the Kinlochewe water, tend to stay at the head of the loch, around the island, the river mouth and the wide bays. This is probably wise, for this area provides the most consistent sport on the loch for both average sized trout and heavyweights. All but the largest lies away down the loch are very difficult to find, even when pointed out. A boat can drift by, only a matter of feet off course, and may as well have missed by a mile.

On Loch Hope, which embodies the rugged beauty of Sutherland, the best fishing is in the top half of the loch which is divided up into Beats 1, 2 and 3 and Middle Bay.

The fishing is run on a rota system from the hotels at Tongue and Altnaharra. There are also estate boats. The holding areas on Hope are rather more numerous than those in the Kinlochewe water of Loch Maree, though not a single one is anything like as large as Maree's head waters. As with the Ross-shire water, Hope has many areas where sea-trout of between 1 and 2 lbs are caught.

Precise boat control is required when passing over the best water on all lochs, though I will hazard that this is rather less important on consistently shallow areas, Beat 1 of Loch Hope, for example, and many of the Hebridean lochs. The lies on such waters are larger and also more variable.

As with all big trout waters, experience is the only key to a continuation of success. Once the lies are discovered it is fatal to pass over them unless a good line of approach is possible, ideally with the right amount of wave and light. Sea-trout are easily frightened and will be 'put down' for the rest of the day if disturbed. Catching them necessitates a campaign in which a fisher must totally immerse himself. During the course of a week one or two truly big fish can be made to move to a fly, and, perhaps, in good conditions, as many as four or five. To achieve this with any consistency, enormous care has to be taken in drawing on many years of stored knowledge and development of the 'instinct'. (Again I am speaking only of highly challenging waters.) But there is probably nothing in fly-fishing which can beat the sight of a colossal trout that has been coaxed into turning over a fly on the surface.

Instead of pursuing a treatise on the art of sea-trout fishing, it would be more enjoyable, at least for me, to give some accounts of representative days that went well, and one or two that went not so well.

The year 1975 was a bad one on the Kinlochewe water.

UDN had ravaged the stocks and though the disease had gone, it was obvious that the trout and salmon were going to take a long time to recover. The loch was high and conditions were ideal. Fish of up to 2 lbs were as numerous as ever, few over 3 lbs had been caught.

One morning I drifted in Dead Tree Bay under a strong wind and heavy rain. Fish were reluctant to move to a bob fly so I began to longline with a slow retrieve. Immediately this brought two sea-trout of about 1¼ lbs to a Black Pennell on the top dropper. The flies were well down in the turbulent water and barely moved as the boat drifted towards them. I remember feeling a slight drag on the line, like a salmon take, and I lifted into a heavy fish deep below the swell. It stayed down and fought doggedly. Was it a salmon or the prize of a good sea-trout? The fish sped beneath the boat. I was over perhaps eighteen feet of water and whatever had been hooked was close to the bottom. The previous season I had had only one good fish that had taken twenty minutes to the net and had turned out to be a 7½-lb salmon. I desperately wanted to boat this fish and find that it was a trout. After five minutes I still had not seen it. He was closer to the surface by then, but was still far off and hidden in the dark water. I turned into the wind to follow him and rain hit my face like a wave; the most refreshing bath you can ever have is in a storm on Maree. Then, quite suddenly, the line trembled and the fish was in the air. It *was* a sea-trout, not enormous, but at 4 lbs it was one of the better fish that year at Kinlochewe – if I could boat it. When there are big trout aplenty they seem to come in easily; when they are scarce the moments are stretched into impossible eternities. Gradually the fish became tired and after what seemed a considerable time, but was in reality about ten minutes, it lay in the net: 4 lbs of spotted gold, with the fly, a Soldier Palmer, tenuously held in the neb of the upper jaw.

That fish should have been enough for me. To my knowledge only two other trout of 4 lbs – and one six-pounder – had been caught that year. The day was young, however, and despite being wet through I persisted into the late evening. Deeper into the bay I caught four more trout through the afternoon, all weighing about 1½ lbs, and all returned to become the giants I might meet in a far-off season.

As the light faded, so the rain relented and the wind dropped. I was drifting into the bay towards the shore. I imagined it, did I not, no more than a shadow among the boulders? I drifted on, watching the place where the figment had flickered; nothing. I shortlined and the top dropper began its hypnotic, furrowing motion; still nothing. Just one more cast, hard against the boulders; it would be the last of the day. The Black Pennell barely surfaced and the shadow I had seen swept over it.

Feeling more relaxed, I fought the fish without nervousness and he came sluggishly to the net. It was nearly dark when it was all over. I weighed my brace of trout that evening, 4 lbs and 5 lbs, and I will always remember the curious mixture of feelings that have grown rather than faded through the years. Elation, thrill, and guilt, for I had killed two good trout when comparable fish were scarce. It was true that I had returned the other six fish I had caught; but those two were lying on the scales, dead. I was aware that something was wrong; something which has nagged at me over the years and has since crystallised into an understanding, the implications of which are discussed in the next chapter.

In July 1977, Jim Mitchell and I were drifting the waters of Loch Hope, on Beat 3. We were quite alone, there were no other boats on the loch. From time to time we saw odd groups of sheep grazing on the lower slopes adjacent to the shore and briefly we glimpsed an eagle through the mist. It was as though there were no other living creatures in the world, apart from ourselves, the sheep and the eagle.

Low clouds were swirling around the hills and by ten in the morning had obscured nearly all of the 3,000 feet of Ben Hope. A gentle wind buffeted us along. Fishing conditions were poor in that dismal light. We were on the edge of a desolate landscape.

Jim was casually fishing the wet fly while I dapped for a change. We had not moved a single fish.

It is odd that for no apparent reason a fisher's instincts will suddenly flare up. It happened on this occasion as I watched the crane-fly I was dapping. It had seemed rather lifeless and the water it covered was as dour and dead as ink. But then I knew, without any doubt whatsoever, that everything had changed. There was a big fish close by, watching the fly. I knew it and yet had seen nothing. Jim told me later that he too had sensed it. Very close to the boat, for the wind had dropped to the merest breeze, the fly hung, its legs caressing the little waves. The awful stillness was abruptly shattered when a salmon rolled out of the deep and took the fly. I let it turn over before I tightened; but I struck into nothing. The fly resurfaced and lay half drowned. Feeling sick with shock and disappointment, I glanced at Jim.

'Did you see . . . ' He went pale as he stared at the bedraggled fly. Suddenly his expression changed. I looked round and saw the fish coming back; a long silver curve. This time I lifted the rod into solid weight.

Salmon rarely give as many problems as big sea-trout. The main concern is their heavier average weight; but this one was unaware of this fact. In a crazed series of leaps and furious, diving runs, it sped across the loch.

Jim is a scientist – we both were in those days – and being interested in statistics he timed the duration of the battle. The leader I was using was 8 lbs breaking strain which I have found to be totally reliable for salmon of up to 15 lbs, and the dapping rod was powerful. After ten minutes the wind picked up and was blowing onshore. Despite this, the salmon held us off and we were pulled for an estimated distance of a quarter of a mile. Throughout the fight the rod was under continuous heavy strain except when the fish leapt, which happened six times. We finally netted it after thirty-six minutes. It was a picture of a salmon; fresh and clean, and it weighed 11 lbs. Without the timing and measurement of the details, the hard facts might have become distorted in my mind over the years; but the proof of the matter was extraordinary. Salmonidae of this calibre are extremely powerful.

I caught one other fish that day, shortly after Jim had boated a sea-trout so fresh that it still had sea-lice on it. Conditions were still working against us. The light had become rather sharp on the eyes and the wind was cold, despite the month. Off Woods Point I rose and hooked a sea-trout that twice tore off fifty yards of backing. Jim timed this battle at twelve minutes and it was no more than we would have expected of a three-pounder. In fact the trout, which also was very fresh, weighed 5½ lbs.

It had been a marvellous day. We returned to Tongue Hotel to weigh the fish. As I stood in front of the scales a French family entered the room. I watched the expression on the face of a little boy of about ten years of age. His eyes widened as he saw the fish I was holding and he fell to his knees and sighed, '*Quel poisson!*' That said it all; the French boy on his knees, the guilty hunter with his prize, silver and heavy in his grasp.

Companions can make or break a day on the water. Just occasionally, the fishing takes second place. July 29th 1981, was one such day when, on the water as elsewhere, the workings of our entire nation ceased as our attention was drawn in another direction.

We would not associate the Fanfare Royale and the Trumpet Voluntary with fly-fishing out on Loch Hope. Neither would we want to under normal circumstances, but on this particular occasion there we were, drifting across the 'Castle' in Middle Bay; our ghillie, affectionately known as the 'Goat', at the oars, and Graeme Longmuir busily trying to keep the radio tuned to the BBC commentary of the Royal Wedding. I was dapping in a feeble westerly, the masterful notes of Sir David Willcocks's orchestra just beginning to take my mind off the fishing. We had just heard that Lady Diana was entering the Cathedral when, whoosh, a two-pounder lurched across the ripple and clipped my fly. I missed it but I could hardly care less. The Goat said that the fish was 6 lbs, although he always says that when we miss one; just to make us feel better!

After that the wind died away even more. We continued to dap, but it was a day for a wedding, not for fishing, and gradually our minds succumbed entirely to the music; we were aware only of London and the happy crowds, of raised trumpets, pomp, and a fairytale come true. It was warm, the flies were moving gently above tiny wavelets. 'Might as well fish in the bath,' announced the Goat. 'Should have stayed at Altnaharra and watched the telly!'

The Royal couple were just leaving St Paul's. With perfect precision and uncanny timing, a sea-trout broached the loch's crinkled surface and engulfed my fly in a porpoising roll away from the boat. It was a classic rise, which at once shattered my reverie and jerked me back to the wild shores of Loch Hope and a racing reel.

Graeme and I begged the Goat to return the fish. It seemed doubly wicked to kill it on such an occasion. 'Put it back, a 2-lb fish,' cried an astonished ghillie; 'I'm in the boat with a couple of madmen! You'll not get many more in that . . . ' He looked out over the glittering loch. The Goat was right; it did not look promising. We saw only one other trout that morning, a splash at Graeme's dap which did no more than shower the fly. But the afternoon held quite different things in store.

We should have known when we collected together for lunch that proceedings later in the day would be a little bizarre. There were six of us gathered on the gravel spit between Beat 3 and Middle Bay; Graeme and Fred, both men of the cloth, two Edinburgh lawyers, the Goat and myself. The purpose of our party was to drink to the newly-weds; and we had come prepared with Union Jacks, gin and champagne. In the process of numerous toasts I acquired a painful stitch as a result of the comic activities of the lawyers – if only their clients could have seen them! When I tried to stand up I discovered what a profound effect the alcohol had had on me. We were all more than a little merry. Even the Goat had a smile across his face which was not produced by any anticipation of good fishing.

I do not remember the return haul up the loch, although I well recall the moment we reached the upwind point of the Goat's favourite bay. 'Ach, the light's not so bad, boys,' he exclaimed. I do not think he could see too clearly: there was a mist on the mountains, a leaden look in the northern sky and a fierce glitter at the head of the loch. 'Get fishing, you daft drunken idiots.' He turned the boat broadside to the swell and I faced into the wind. Something was wrong but I could not grasp what it was. 'Er, Jeremy,' the Goat whispered carefully, 'why don't you turn around and face the right way?' Graeme started to chuckle and that set me off. Soon we were laughing uncontrollably at every derisive comment which the Goat could throw our way. I could not see my fly but I vaguely hoped that it was out there on the surface and not suspended ten feet above the tumbling waves.

Soon after passing the Point I became aware of something splashing off to my left. I looked at Graeme and noticed that his rod was bending and bucking violently. I finally realised that he was attached to a sea-trout which was rather unhappy about the situation. I informed him with utmost sincerity that he was, in fact, into a fish. Another thunderclap of laughter came by way of reply. Graeme was absolutely unaware of what was happening. The Goat was almost frantic now as he persuaded Graeme to bring the trout around the back of the boat. I was doubled up with laughter and my stitch had come back. Through streaming tears I watched the ensuing battle. I was brought back to a degree of sobriety by an unfriendly thumping through my rod. In astonishment I looked around to realise that I too had hooked a sea-trout. With more luck than judgment, both fish were boated before Graeme and myself finally collapsed on our backs, writhing hysterically and yet no sound escaping from our oxygen-starved lungs. The Goat just sat there, ribald comments now exhausted, shaking his head in total disbelief.

It was a good five minutes before we were again fit to hold the rods steady and recommence dapping. In fact the conditions were perfect for wet fly, but in our hopeless state that was out of the question. I remember a quick silver flash beneath my fly, though I should not have been looking, because I failed to connect. Graeme must have had his eyes shut, however, for soon he had another two-and-a-half-pounder in the boat.

The wind picked up and rolled the chuckling waters. Our alcohol-induced absurdity waned in pace with the rise of the fish. We started to pack up as the Goat guided our boat back to its moorings. The point of this tale is that sea-trout and men can, at times, be of equal intelligence, and both have a sense of occasion!

Loch Hope worked its magic on me again; I had been given unparalleled enjoyment with rod and line on the powerful pitching waters of that lonely strath. Each time the experience is different. Often we ride across the waves where lilac backs arch briefly before the mind's eye can sufficiently capture the burst of animal motion. Often the fish are scarce; but we are left with the primordial expanse of the north, and our companions who add a human dimension to what might otherwise be intolerable loneliness.

When pursuing sea-trout, besides having a balanced team, there is nothing as important as the speed at which we move the flies through the water. The 'shortlining triangle' which I described in the last chapter allows the flies to be worked extremely slowly and, if necessary, with barely any movement at all. Longlining, also, lends itself to the slow retrieve. I can think of very few sea-trout weighing over 4 lbs that I have taken on a quickly moved fly. As with brown trout, the reason for sea-trout rising 'short' is nearly always because of a fly which is too large or one which is fished too fast. Remember, we are considering sea-trout in lochs, not the fish fresh from the salt whose instincts are still directed towards attacking sand-eels. A team consisting entirely of bright attractors, such as may be put up when fresh trout are abundant, *might* be better if it is fished faster than a more conventional arrangement.

Having said this, the pattern of fly is not insignificant, particularly with regard to balance. I have listed faithful patterns in the Appendix. They are mostly well-known patterns but my own dressings differ from shop-bought ones in terms of the angles at which the wings are set, materials used for the bodies, lengths of tails and hackles, and so on. The Mallard and Claret I use in one set of conditions might be quite a different fly from the one I put up in a different situation. Furthermore, those patterns that I have found successful might in other hands be useless, and vice versa. I know several fishers, for example, who find the Butcher a deadly fly for sea-trout, whereas I hate it. To me it looks all wrong and seems to upset the balance of any team I use. I tend to use bushier or more translucent patterns on droppers and slim, opaque flies on the tail.

It is an amusing and usually inexplicable phenomenon in fly-fishing that trout occasionally find one pattern exclusively attractive. On Loch Hope in 1978 and 1979 I discovered the effectiveness of a peculiar looking fly called the Camasunary Killer which originated, as its name implies, in Camasunary in Skye. (This fly was designed by Stephen Johnson and is described in his book *Fishing From Afar*.) For those two seasons this pattern on a size 10 hook attracted almost half the total number of sea-trout I took from Hope. On some days they would move to nothing else. I found that it worked well in various teams and was best in the middle position. My experiences with this fly were consolidated in 1980 on Loch Maree. That year was, in fact, a vintage one for me. In a week at Kinlochewe, when I was not even fishing every day, I caught fifty-two sea-trout, five of which were over 5 lbs in weight and the best was just under 7 lbs. Eight others weighed over 3 lbs. On one of those days alone the Camasunary fly attracted fourteen of the sixteen trout caught. Yet in the seasons since then, though I have used this fly often on various lochs, the only place it has done anywhere near as well as during those strange years was in the Hebrides, where, frankly, almost any fly would have worked!

The 1981 season on Maree was peculiar. After the

previous classic season, low water either kept much of the stock of sea-trout out in Loch Ewe or made them reluctant to move to the fly until the coming of the rains and cooler water in September. I met three Irish fishers who were visiting the loch for the first time. They had had a modicum of success with a small Green Peter, but had caught virtually nothing on any other fly. During a particularly dour day of feeble wind on the loch I tried one of these flies that I had been given, putting it in the middle position. Green is a colour that rarely has its day with sea-trout on north-western lochs; much of the time it appears to be unattractive. Sandwiched between a Blue-Silver and a Pennell, the Green Peter did not look right, but it began to grow on me because I could see that the fish liked it very much indeed. Since then it has been successful on only a few occasions, always fished very slowly on a long line. But it has never achieved the same impact on sea-trout as on those few days. Perhaps the copies of the fly that I have tied since then have lacked the magic of those Irish dressers!

Thinking about flies from 'across the water', reminds me of Kingsmill Moore's *A Man May Fish*. Concerned with Irish brown and sea-trout, he made a study of certain colours which he considered to be highly attractive to trout, despite a scarcity of those particular colours in nature. Thus the royal blue of the Camasunary, the vivid emerald of the Green Peter and the lovely intensity of Kingsmill Moore's own Claret Bumble all have their day for trout and sea-trout. But shape and form are as important as colour, perhaps more so. Judging by the translucence and essential insect character of some of Kingsmill Moore's favoured patterns, evidently he too knew this.

It was also in 1981 that I met up with one of the two, possibly three, sea-trout that I have encountered weighing more than 10 lbs. At about nine in the morning in a southerly wind, Jim and I were drifting past the island at the head of Maree where there is a weed bed stretching out on a long reef away from the island. At one particular point on the edge of these weeds is a very good lie for big sea-trout. The rest of the bed teems with finnock and smaller sea-trout. Jim had never before fished this holding area. As we drifted on the pleasant breeze, I pointed to a hole at the edge of the weed twenty yards ahead of us. I gave a pull on the downwind oar so that we would drift over the spot I had indicated. 'I had a five-pounder there last year, right where the flies are now. And the year before – oh my God!' As I spoke, the giant was on the surface, coming straight at us. His head, most of his back and the top of what was a huge tail were in the air. Instinct told me what to do; I kept the rod up, holding the fly at the surface, just stroking it along. A rod's length out from the boat, the enormous trout accelerated, closed his mouth and clipped the fly with his nose as he turned downwards, and he was gone. I sat there stunned. Jim poured a cup of coffee and lit me a cigarette. 'That was it, Jim,' I said weakly, 'the fish of a lifetime, and I moved the fly just that bit too fast.' Gaelic speakers would have called it '*Mhor Breac*', a great trout. It was certainly that.

In calm weather, shortlining becomes useless. The loch lies flat or barely ruffled by a feeble breeze. Both dapping and the classic loch style require only a gentle wind; but there comes a time when neither method has much chance of success. It is then essential to longline, using either a single dry fly, which is ideal for fresh or small sea-trout, or two small wet flies on a long leader. In calm weather the most severe problem is overcoming the disturbance created by a fisher as he casts and retrieves. The flies should be sparsely dressed so that they cut through the surface film and the leader should be thoroughly cleaned with soap so that it does not float. The knots in particular need to be worked on with a mixture of Fuller's earth and soap because they have a nasty habit of floating and forming a fish-scaring wake during the retrieve. (Neutral density lines are becoming popular for such conditions, while an undressed Kingfisher silk was perfection.) This slow long-lining is akin to nymph fishing, and though calm weather always presents difficulties it is surprising how often the method works. There is a wonderful sense of achievement in taking good sea-trout on any fly method; but in a flat calm or slightly rippled water, it is more than satisfying to feel the sudden whirl of a big fish and then to see the mirror of the loch's surface shatter twenty-five yards away. In conditions such as this one is more likely to take finnock or small sea-trout, unless the larger fish are fresh from the sea. On light tackle, however, a 12-oz finnock is a sporting fish, and there is no better meal.

One of the best presents anyone ever gave me was a fishing log. Before this I had always kept some sort of record of noteworthy days, but so much is lost in the recess of one's memory. The log serves as a reminder and it gives me enormous pleasure to sit by the fire on a winter's evening, flicking through the pages. With the help of accurate details we can relive the battles, the humorous occasions, the days of huge catches and blanks, and odd fish that came from nowhere. We feel again the warm, wet Atlantic storms and the heavy heat of August days. Turning the pages through the years, we see again the deer and the mountain goats, the eagle and the falcon. We watch the rowan berries ripen and the silver birch rustling and turning gold in autumn winds; but most of all we feel again the rod bending into big sea-trout. Searching through my log, I vividly recall the last week in September 1985 at Loch Maree. It is a perfect example of an average but challenging week's fishing under a mixture of conditions.

Since the first runs in June there had been plenty of rain and the sea-trout had pushed up from Loch Ewe in good numbers. Fishers had suffered, however, from a lack of good fishing conditions up at Kinlochewe. My first day there was a rarity, with a good, consistent wind from the south-east, broken cloud bringing a little rain, and a few sunny spells. At dawn I drifted under drogue out towards the island in Dead Tree Bay. For the first two hours the wind was a little strong, so I fished a long line using my ten-foot rod and size 8 and 10 flies. On the first drift I rose four fish by the island, hooking two of them, but losing them after a few seconds. I was retrieving too fast. Throughout that drift I had noticed several trout on the surface away to my left. I rowed the boat into the bay and drifted over the area where I had seen those fish. Within a few casts I had the first trout in the boat, soon followed by another; both weighed about 1¼ lbs. I was barely moving the flies and the trout were now taking with confidence. In water about eighteen feet deep, mid-way between the shore and the island, a big fish went for the top dropper seconds after it had landed. I waited a moment before tightening. About 250 yards away from where I hooked that trout – on the far side of the island – I boated him. As the net engulfed the big fish the fly fell out of his mouth. If I had delayed another second I am sure I would have lost him. He weighed exactly 5 lbs. On the next drift I boated another weighing 2¾ lbs. I packed up and went in for a late breakfast.

If the morning had been good because of the two heavy fish, the afternoon was spectacular in terms of numbers. Farther up the loch, on the north-east shore, the wind was blowing from the south, having 'curved' around the vast rock mass of Slioch. Using the same team that had been so successful in the morning, I shortlined over a single, slow drift from Pine Tree Bay to the White Stone, and brought twenty-seven rises to the bob fly. I boated fourteen sea-trout of between 1 and 2 lbs and six finnock.

It had been a day of rather easy fishing, largely because the conditions had been perfect. But easy days teach us relatively little; they simply serve to consolidate old knowledge.

The following day was Tuesday, and conditions had changed, being flat calm for most of the day. It was a time for exploring with a long line and two small wet flies. Leaving the big fish lies alone, I was well rewarded with three sea-trout of average size and four finnock. All these took a lot more 'catching' than those of the previous day.

On the Wednesday the wind picked up slightly and I drifted the south-western shore, shortlining when the breeze flicked up the water, longlining when the wind fell. Quiet spells followed sudden bursts of activity. In the heavy dusk off Grudie Point I finished the day with six sea-trout, one brown trout and five finnock. I moved a monster of a fish off one of the points up the loch but it did not take the fly.

If Tuesday had been difficult, Thursday was as impossible as it could be for sea-trout. The loch was like a mirror and the sun glared relentlessly from both sky and water. I saw only one sea-trout within range on the surface in several hours' fishing. I put a dry fly where he had risen and he wolfed it down immediately. He was a good fish and I was lucky to have caught him in those conditions. In the afternoon I struggled long and hard for three finnock. The day was rather inconsequential as far as the fishing went, but good for a sun-tan.

Friday was perhaps the best day of all, not in terms of the number of fish caught, but because of the challenging conditions. Once again there was little wind. This was my last day on the loch and I was desperate for one more good trout. I thought there might be a slender chance of a take on one of the holding points where a slack wind was cutting little ripples on the water. In a faint, rather eerie light, I was surprised to take four fresh trout of between 1¼ and 1½ lbs. Time was running out and the wind was falling. I knew it would be calm again in a matter of minutes. It looked like dusk out there, although it was only five in the afternoon. If there were any good fish about they would be in shallow water, so often the haunt of trout in late evening. I cast towards the shore where the water was no more than a foot deep; the tail fly almost hit the grey stones on the beach. The surface suddenly bulged, and I was into a wolf of a trout. He fought fiercely and, though he weighed only 3 lbs, in a better year he might have been 6 lbs. Moreover, he was the most perfect, heavily marked cock fish I have ever seen. He meant rather more to me than Monday's five-pounder. In fact I considered him to be my 'fish of the year'. Perhaps only a sea-trout fisher will understand that; the true value of our sport is not measured in pounds and ounces.

It is now quite some time since that week in September and the sea-trout are on the redds in early winter, the fly-fisher far away. But in summers to come the drawn-out days will once again stir the deep-seated instincts. And during long nights in England, before he takes to the roads leading north, the fisher's thoughts travel before him, recapturing the beauty of the mountains, dragging sleep away and leaving him restless in the darkness. His eyes stare into space and he sees only the vision of sea-trout in tumbling waters and the dancing dropper flies on the surface. He is set apart from other men, cut off from civilisation, his mind vibrant, like quick fins. A single word passes his lips: Maree.

9

The Way Ahead

THE FUTURE OF the lochs is blurred, and the continuance of fly-fishing for wild trout is in question. In the hills the brown trout is probably safe, apart from one major threat: acidification. Sport fishing in the high country puts minimal pressure on the natural stock; there are so many lochs and countless trout. The acid rain that is destroying the lakes and forests of Scandinavia and eastern Europe is already beginning to take its toll on Scottish fisheries where there is little calcium-rich rock to buffer its effects. The fly-fisher is relatively powerless to prevent this. Only governments can move to protect our wild places and, against the short-term economic gains of industrialisation, what chance has the lonely hill loch?

In yet more danger are the sea-trout and salmon fisheries, which are being assaulted from all sides. Migratory salmonidae are valuable, and their tremendous resilience to exploitation has long since been fatigued. The salmon, in particular, is rapidly approaching the endangered list, at least in its wild state. The mysterious sea-trout will have a similar fate. Even on the greatest of our lochs, as fly-fishers know only too well, the heavy fish are not nearly as plentiful as they were two decades ago. Acidification is damaging the sensitive breeding redds, while commercial poaching and inshore and offshore netting are causing nothing short of havoc among adult fish.

There is a faint chance that the wild migrant stocks may eventually be preserved. Salmon farming of captive fish is becoming increasingly widespread in Scottish and Irish inshore waters. As more and more of these fish reach the fishmongers, so the commercial value of the wild creature falls. In the end it is hoped that the exploitation of natural stocks will become uneconomic. The law courts are gradually waking up to the effects illegal fishing is having on salmonidae. Indeed, the future of wild fish stocks largely depends on increased powers of water bailiffs and the increased severity of legal penalties for offenders. The courts may succeed, at this late hour, in destroying this menace of illegal fishing.

The English lakes are relatively safe, but not necessarily as fly-only waters or even trout fisheries. The stocking of farmed trout in carefully monitored water supplies has been a success for thirty years and continues to improve.

Fly-fishing faces the way ahead in a make or break situation. We are now in the dawn of a radical movement which seeks to preserve the art form in the sport. Fishers of the classic and imitative styles are on the increase and are finding aesthetic values in the sport beyond compare. It remains to be seen whether or not this movement survives against the counter-attitude that the weight of a creel at the day's end, achieved by any method within the rules, is all that matters.

Fishery managements in England alone hold the key. It

is within their power to develop fly-fishing or largely to destroy it by allowing certain methods and base principles to banish the magic from our stillwaters.

Rules have tended, these past twenty years, to have been broadened so that short-term gains can be achieved – the rapid capture of big trout for the sake of publicity, both for fisheries and fishing notorieties. I have seen the development of some of the trout-fisher personalities of today and I have witnessed the enormous detrimental effects they have had on the sport. The 'hype', the advertising and the self-perpetuating system they have created have launched them towards heights of dominance where they remain largely unchallenged. But I do take up the challenge, for I passionately believe in the value of our beautiful waters as trout fisheries and I will seek to protect them as far as I am able.

Some of these men who have appointed themselves as the angling 'shepherds' are doing a tremendous disservice to our sport. Few fly-fishers notice that to make their heavy catches they exist on the edge of the rules. They bypass the mainstream of principles that is part of the sport's inner strength. Water authorities, managements, the tackle trade and the press have often encouraged such behaviour. Waters become famous as a result of good catches. The angling press needs its headlines, the trade needs custom . . . The degenerating system is cheap, in both senses of the word, but self-supporting.

Alongside the treasured guiding influences in our sport, men such as Arthur Cove, are others, in large numbers, who have inverted and confused fly-fishing principles for two decades, perhaps longer, for personal gain or the necessity of feeding shallow egos. At a time when so many things threaten our waters and the sport itself, we should be furious at any influence which seeks to denigrate what should be the most artistic and fulfilling out-of-doors activity that mankind has devised.

In Scotland the fishery controllers face a more difficult task. Acid rain is likely mercilessly to wash away all their efforts. But, assuming that a government more caring of long-term issues takes office, we can hope that acidification will be curbed. The preservation of wild stocks and the natural environment is of immeasurable importance. If this can be done with the help of fish-farming techniques then so be it. We must take care, however, for we might as well fish for the highly-naturalised stock of a southern English lake as for cage-reared sea-trout in the Highlands. There is little difference. The creature that has known only redd, river, loch and sea is a priceless work of nature's art.

So far as the sport is concerned, there is much the individual can do. It takes a long time to escape our sheep-like following of a quantitative goal and subjectively to pursue a more skilful approach; although with the acceptance of this simple philosophy a vast arena opens within the bounds of self-imposed limitations.

The principles of 'catch and return' are well understood. In the last chapter I spoke of a strange feeling when killing large trout when they are scarce. This has troubled me through the years, but I have now reached a compromise. Provided a trout or salmon is undamaged and is not too tired after being caught, there is every reason to believe that it will survive if returned. On fisheries where this is done as a matter of course, it has been shown that casualties are exceptional. (Consider, for example, the American Gold Medal waters, or, closer to home, that splendid little fishery at Tenterden, Kent.) The fly-fisher following this practice has to make some adjustments in his thinking. It is extremely cruel to allow a fish to fight to the point of exhaustion, then to manhandle it in the net and to rip out a large, barbed hook before throwing it back into the water. When a fisher is concerned for his quarry, his actions are quite different. Barbless hooks are wonderful things. Provided that they do not penetrate a major blood-vessel in the fish's mouth, any wounds they produce will rapidly heal. Furthermore, I am convinced that we lose a negligible number of trout as a result of barbless flies. If the correct tension is applied to rod and line during the fight, there is no reason why any well set hook should come loose. I have used barbless and reduced-barb hooks for salmon, sea-trout, brown and rainbow trout for several seasons and have every faith in them. (Take care, however; the design of hook is important here; I use the hooks listed in Chapter 4. I break off the barbs by squeezing them with pliers, or I file them down with a sharpening stone. These hooks are utterly reliable; many are not.)

Once the fish is netted, the fly can easily be withdrawn. Smaller trout need not even be netted. You can feel down the line for the fly, grip it between finger and thumb and twist it loose.

A knotless, seamless landing net – these are readily available – is kinder to the fish than the conventional type, causing little abrasion to scales or mucous coat. The fish need never be held by hand at all. A little pressure on a gill cover while the trout lies in the net-mesh in the bottom of the boat or on the grass is sufficient to hold the fish still while the hook is extracted. While in the net it can be lowered gently into the water and freed, perhaps no worse than a little wiser for its experience. It is essential that the fish be returned quickly, certainly in less than a minute after netting. A trout out of water for longer than this has little chance of pulling through: he may swim off, but will probably die later. With practice, the whole procedure from netting to return can be accomplished in fifteen to twenty seconds. If required, weighing can be done while the fish is 'in the mesh', by subtracting the weight of the wet net. This takes no longer than ten seconds. If the trout is obviously damaged or if the hook is difficult to remove, then simply kill the fish in the time-honoured manner with no perpetuation of suffering.

During the last eight seasons, I have not killed a single salmon that I have caught – the eleven-pounder which I described in Chapter 8 was the last of my victims – and I also make a point of returning hen brown and sea-trout. (Even relatively young cock fish become sexually mature rather early and can fertilise the ova on the redds.) I kill a reasonable number of finnock and sea-trout weighing up to 1½ lbs, for they are superb eating and just because I kill them myself makes it no worse than any of us who eat meat and fish.

I hope this book is rather more than an account of how to catch trout in stillwaters. Many so-called 'experts' can tell us how to do that. Instead, I have described my own composite approach to trout and the beautiful loch and lake environments where we find them. I believe that the classic and imitative styles are the only ways in which we can hunt this magnificent animal without offending too deeply the principles of moral man. A dead fish might be just a dead fish; but to the fly-fisher who has caught a trout by blending skill and instinct it becomes an invaluable prize. And if that trout is returned unharmed to the loch it is the most precious prize of all; once held, now given back to nature.

The rod bends and the line stretches straight as far off, in deep water, a big trout feels the strain at his head. It is best of all, I suspect, when he blasts out into the loch and the fly tears loose and he is free.

Appendix

BELOW IS A SUMMARY of fly patterns which are of considerable use to the fly-fisher pursuing the styles discussed in this book.

Nymphs

The **Cove Pheasant Tail** should be dressed in sizes ranging from 14 to 8. Cock pheasant tail fibres are wound on the hook shank, buzzer fashion. The rib is medium copper wire. The thorax consists of a ball of dubbed rabbit fur, including the guard hairs well teased out. The wing case is formed from pheasant tail fibres. The quality of this fly may be altered by many factors such as colour of the pheasant fibres used, width of copper wire, thickness of the dubbed rabbit, to mention but a few. I dress the standard form as well as many minor variations so that the pattern more closely represents certain food forms like corixae or shrimp. One can produce quite specialised versions simply by the choice of pheasant colour or length of the rabbit thorax. The modes of dressing this pattern are as versatile as the ways in which it may be presented.

The **buzzers** are the multitude species of chironomid of which there must have been thousands of different imitations. Simplicity, as so often, is the key, although it is as well to have a variation in size and colour. Without doubt the chironomids are more important than any other food form to trout in stillwaters. My own series of buzzers has offered me consistent service and yet took me several years to develop (in terms of the fine details). On size 14, 12 and 10 hooks I dub wool of the required colour on the abdomen in the accepted style, fairly closely ribbed with silver lurex. The thorax consists of wool of the same colour as the abdomen (for the emerald green and claret versions I use peacock herl which more closely represents the dark thorax of the species which these patterns attempt to mimic). To express the breathing filaments I dub in some white wool at the hook eye. It is extraordinary the difference that dubbing makes to this area of the fly when compared with the flatness of the more conventional piece of floss. By far the most important body colours are black, pale green, emerald and claret. Peter Grundel is fond of a red version which can be particularly useful in coloured water. The Orange–Silver imitation is rather special. This insect is not so brightly coloured as one might think. It is essentially grey with a distinct shine and possessing variable bands of colour that are light red or dark orange. A wonderful representation is as follows. A tail of white floss or wool is tied in, followed by red and amber tying silk wound and tapered up the abdomen around the bend. This is ribbed closely with silver lurex. The thorax is dubbed rabbit with just a touch of dark orange wool. White wool is again dubbed at the head. My hatching buzzer I have described in the text. It differs from the standard range only in that the abdomen is entirely silver. The various species of ginger, brown and golden dun buzzers can easily be represented by carefully chosen pheasant tails, or the wingless gold-ribbed hare's ear.

The **Green Nymph** is a general pattern which is particularly useful in cloudy or weedy water, or when trout are feeding on small food forms such as daphnia, tiny buzzers or caenis. The colour and texture of the wool is the problem as, to my knowledge, it can only be obtained in Orkney. The closest copy I have found – and it is successful – is Anchor T3134. On a size 10 or 8 hook the wool is dubbed, slightly around the hook bend. A short tail of cock pheasant is preferred by the fly's inventor, Peter Grundel. The thin abdomen is tightly ribbed with gold lurex. The thorax is dressed with the same wool, slightly thicker than the abdomen, and a wing case of cock pheasant is pulled over the thorax. Peter likes also to tie in a few 'legs' of cock pheasant.

The **Amber Sedge Pupa** is another of Peter Grundel's patterns and is tremendously successful at sedge time. A beautifully simple dressing on 12 or 10 hooks, the body is divided into two parts. The abdomen, the longest part, is amber seal fur substitute, while the thorax is rabbit fur. Both abdomen and thorax are dubbed fairly finely and both are covered over the top of the dressing by cock pheasant. The colour of the abdomen material can, of course, be altered for a closer match to specific naturals. Dull and pale green are useful alternatives. Do not be put off when this nymph becomes ragged and torn by trouts' teeth. It is then even more deadly, like so many flies.

As well as those truly essential nymphs mentioned above, it is wise to have a few for more occasional use. The **Bloodworm**, in bright red, is a nymph I sometimes use when the trout are hard on the bottom or at the base of weed beds, gorging themselves on these creatures, which can easily be an inch long. Despite the length of some of these larvae they can be imitated easily enough with 'fly-size' hooks. I use a 10 or 8 and tie in a reasonable length of floss as a tail. I wind more floss thinly up the shank and rib widely with fine gold braid. A tiny thorax of peacock herl finishes the fly. The secret is to aim for an extremely sparse imitation, the naturals being little thicker than a hook. I fish the larva over deep water on very long leaders. The trick is to barely retrieve at all unless there is weed on the bed. Then only the occasional twitch should be given to the line.

The bright, dashing **corixae** species are simple to imitate. Essentially we tie a short dressing on a 12 or 10 hook. The body can be white floss or wool, closely ribbed with silver lurex. I like to add a tag of silver to represent that all-important air bubble that corixae carry. A wing case of dark pheasant tail and two long arms of the same fibre, sloping slightly backwards to represent the corixa's swimming legs, completes the fly. Sink and draw this pattern in shallow and weedy water during summer and autumn. A rapid rise to the surface induces explosive reactions from hunting trout. Some species of corixae have distinctive yellow or olive colouring. A little wool in the body or wing case produces the desired effect. For very dark species there is no better imitation than a long-thoraxed pheasant tail.

Very large nymphs such as Damsel and Mayfly might suggest the need for a long-shanked hook. As I have said, I never use these. Neither is there a need. For the **Damsel** nymph I use a hook size of 10 or 8. I dress in a long tail of pale green wool and three pheasant tail fibres. I dub a mixture of the same pale green wool and olive seal fur substitute as an abdomen, ribbed with gold lurex. The thorax is a thick bunch (this is one of a very few patterns that benefits from a bit of bulk) of the olive fur. The wing case is the usual pheasant. A thin hackle of brown or grey partridge is an attractive extra. This pattern drifts high in the water. I do not fish the Damsel nymph deep. I like to cast it out on a fairly long leader without droppers. I allow it to drift, giving occasional long draws towards the bank.

For the **Mayfly** nymph I use a similar method of dressing, but tie instead the expected cream, pale yellow and buff wools in the required mixture. I also add fairly long legs fashioned in pheasant tail. There are very few lakes in England nowadays which have a reasonable mayfly population. When a hatch occurs, however, trout will invariably become preoccupied. (It would be ridiculous, one should add, for a fisher to be in western Ireland in June without an adequate supply of mayfly, both nymph and dry.)

Dry Flies

As a general representation of **olives**, the **Greenwell's Glory** is magnificent. Dark olives might best be imitated by using olive, rather than the usual primrose, silk in the body dressing.

The **Dry Buzzers** I have already described in the text; the black, emerald or amber bodied forms, ribbed with gold or silver lurex and hackled with black, badger or red-game respectively, yield imitations which cover all needs, in hook sizes 14–10.

The simple **Red Palmer**, on a 12 or 10 hook, is a splendid starting point at **sedge** time. The fly consists simply of a Palmered body of red-game, ribbed with gold, and a slightly thicker head hackle. I vary the colour of the hackles used, to achieve different shades and colours, in order to yield closer copies of the active naturals. A roof-shaped wing of hen pheasant (again vary the colour and shade) affords a more visible and life-like pattern.

I fish a **Snail** imitation as a dry fly, in the surface film. I dress a bulky **Black and Peacock Spider**, adding an underbody of black wool. The hackle I choose is stiff and short, and I trim it shorter. If only the hackles are greased the 'Snail' hangs enticingly in the film.

A short-hackled **Coch-y-bondhu** is fine for imitating the **soldier and sailor beetles** that find their way into stillwaters.

The Black and Amber Dry Buzzers, already described, unribbed, yield adequate representations of **black and red ants**, falls of which sometimes occur in hot weather. It is quite unnecessary, but I like to dress these ants with a more correctly shaped body, fashioned from black or amber tying silk which I then varnish to produce the shine of the natural.

Caenis are not as difficult to imitate as they are to fish effectively. I tie a white hackled and bodied fly with a short white tail, using amber tying silk, on a size 14 hook. A double version of this fly sometimes works, i.e. with a hackle and tail at both ends of the shank; although success with direct imitations of caenis is always limited.

The **hawthorn fly** can sometimes be blown on to stillwaters. A good pattern consists of black wool or feather fibre wound on to the hook shank (size 12 or 10), slightly around the bend. The characteristic hind legs of this insect are represented by two long, knotted, black feather fibres tied in under the dressing, sloping backwards and down. A wing of any stiff grey feather, rolled, is tied in and a black hackle wound at the head. The closely related **heather fly**, found as the name implies in heathery country, is similarly imitated, the only difference being a hackle of dark red-game, or Rhode Island red.

Drone flies vary in size and colour. The famous Grafham drone has not appeared in any numbers for more than ten years. When these strange insects do appear an imitation fished in the surface is desirable. I dub alternate bands of amber and brown wool (varying in shade depending on the colours of the natural) on to the abdomen of a 10 or 8 hook. I then tie two white cock hackle tips sloping back over the body. The dressing is completed with a red-game hackle.

The **Crane-Fly** is the most important of all the windfalls. These large insects induce all species of trout to rise, even large sea-trout. My own version consists of a dressing on a size 8 hook, incorporating cock pheasant tail for the abdomen, ribbed with fine gold braid. Six legs (the number does not matter; I am sure trout cannot count) are formed from knotted strands of pheasant tail tied in under the body and sloping backwards. The head hackle can be either red-game, honey or furnace. I rarely bother with wings nowadays, but when I do they are formed from pale game hackle tips, dressed spent.

The **white dry fly** I mention in the text is useful whenever **moths** abound on summer evenings. I find it is even more effective when trout are attacking **fry** in the shallows. On a number 10 hook I dress in a tail of a few strands of white ostrich herl. I then form a body from the same material and rib with silver lurex. A short-fibred badger cock hackle at the head completes the fly. Just as when fishing the snail, only the hackle should be greased with this fly. It lies almost inert in the surface, its tail hanging down.

Traditional Wet Flies

The dressings of these I will not give. Being traditional patterns, their structures are available in many other books.* I suggest, however, that a rigorous adherence to the exact pattern is unnecessary. Materials in contemporary use are usually more translucent and 'vital' than the flat silk and over-hackled originals. Furthermore, one can dress a Mallard and Claret, say, in several different ways, varying wing angle, tail length, shade of body material etc. A tailor-made fly for a particular set of circumstances or conditions might bear little resemblance to one bought over the counter. None the less, the flies in the following list are ones in which I have total confidence, always bearing in mind the concept of a team, the conditions, time of year and the quarry.

My favourites are as follows: Black Pennell, Claret Pennell, Soldier Palmer, Black and Peacock Spider, Cinnamon and Gold, Invicta, Whickham's Fancy, Grenadier, Greenwell's Glory, March Brown (standard and silver versions), Teal and Green (I prefer this to the Green Peter mentioned in the text), Ginger and Dark Quills. For fresh sea-trout I would certainly add the Camasunary Killer and the Blue Zulu. I regard all of these as dropper patterns. The Mallard and Claret, Peter Ross and Teal and Orange (the latter at sedge time) are excellent tail flies.

This list is not regarded as comprehensive. It has simply served me well over the years as it has been developed.

---

* For accurate dressing details one should refer to Courtney Williams: *A Dictionary of Trout Flies* or Tom Stewart's series on the subject. On stillwater flies in general Goddard's *Trout Flies of Stillwater* remains the best comprehensive work available. See Bibliography.

Bibliography

Bridgett, R.C., *Loch-Fishing in Theory and Practice*, Herbert Jenkins, 1924.

Goddard, John, *Trout Flies of Stillwater*, A & C Black, 1969.

Johnson, Stephen, *Fishing From Afar*, Peter Davies, 1947.

—— *Fishing With a Purpose*, Peter Davies, 1969.

McLaren, Charles C., *Art of Sea-Trout Fishing*, Oliver & Boyd, 1963.

Moore, T.C. Kingsmill, *A Man May Fish*, Herbert Jenkins, 1960.

Oatts, Col. H.A., *Loch Trout*, Herbert Jenkins, 1958.

Sawyer, Frank, *Nymphs and the Trout*, A & C Black, 1958.

Spencer, Sidney, *Newly From the Sea*, Witherby, 1969.

—— *Salmon and Sea-Trout in Wild Places*, Witherby, 1968.

Stewart, Tom, *50 Popular Flies* (4 vols), Ernest Benn, 1962, 1964, 1969, 1973.

Walker, C.F., *Lake Flies and their Imitation*, Herbert Jenkins, 1960.

Williams, A. Courtney, *A Dictionary of Trout Flies*, A & C Black, 1949.